MOMENTS

WITH

GOD

MOMENTS
WITH
GOD

BY NNEKA DEAN

Guided and written by the

Holy Spirit

Table of Contents

INTRODUCTION 1

I.   BE STILL AND KNOW 5

II.   OBEDIENCE OVER SACRIFICE 9

III.   FROM TOP TO BOTTOM 13

IV.   DOERS AND NOT HEARERS ONLY.......17

V.   LOVE THE LORD YOUR GOD 21

VI.   THE LORD IS 25

VII.   BEGINNING OF WISDOM.......................27

VIII.   GOD IS LOVE 29

IX.   WORSHIP IN SPIRIT AND TRUTH 31

X.   GUARD YOUR HEART AND EYES 35

XI.   HARDEN NOT YOUR HEART 39

XII.   THAT MAN SHOULD BE ALONE...........43

XIII.   PRODUCTION OF CHARACTER............47

XIV.   PLANTED BY THE WATER 53

XV.   70 X 7..57

XVI.   SEARCH ME, O GOD AND KNOW 61

XVII.   AS FOR ME 65

XVIII.   MEANT IT FOR GOOD...........................69

XIX.   CAST THE FIRST STONE 73

XX.   PRAY WITHOUT CEASING............... 77

XXI.   NOT BY MIGHT, NOR BY POWER 81

XXII.   DIRECT MY STEPS 85

XXIII.   NEW WINE 89

XXIV.   LOVE COVERS 93

XXV.   ABIDE 97

XXVI.   CLEAN & NEW HEART 101

XXVII.   PEACE BE STILL 105

XXVIII.   IN ALL THINGS 109

XXIX.   CAST YOUR CARES 113

XXX.   REMEMBER ME 117

XXXI.   LION AND THE LAMB..................... 121

XXXII.   A HIDDEN TREASURE 125

XXXIII.   IN THE BEGINNING 129

XXXIV.   GOD WITH US 133

XXXV.   FOR GOD SO LOVED THE WORLD.. 137

EXPLANATION OF REFERENCED VERSES 141

INTRODUCTION

Writing this devotional has been a true work of ministry for me. The Lord has guided me through every step of this process. I have never written a book before, nor did I have a guideline or an idea for how to go about writing one, so taking on this venture has been an act of true surrender, faith and obedience for me. I'm not someone who has an official background in writing and I didn't go to school to study the Bible. I'm simply a woman who loves the Lord and genuinely wants to share with everyone and anyone who will listen to the truth about the goodness of God.

First and foremost, I want to give credit and honor where it is due. Every devotional heading in this book has been paraphrased or partially quoted from scripture found in the Bible. It was the Holy Spirit who reminded me of these different verses and sat with me in quiet contemplation of God's Word. In those moments, He gave me fresh revelations of the meaning of God's Word and how it can be applied to our own lives. Since it was the Holy Spirit leading and guiding me through this journey, I thought it was only right to acknowledge His hand in the creation of this book.

This book is titled "Moments with God," because each devotional was birthed from being led to a particular scripture, spending time meditating over the meaning of that scripture, and then asking and allowing the Lord to speak and reveal anything He wanted to through that verse. This would often lead to Him revealing how much of His Word compliments itself. Looking at one scripture would lead me to uncover how it connected to other scriptures in the Bible and how they all worked together to reveal the beauty and truth of God's Word.

My prayer for anyone who reads this book is that you are able to have these moments with God, where you find yourself being renewed, refreshed, encouraged, and reminded of the things of God. May He speak to you and also give you personal, specific revelations of who He is, who you are in Him & how spending even one moment with God is worth more than a thousand moments doing anything else. With each encounter, may you find yourself wanting to go deeper and spend even more time with Him.

Lastly, I want to encourage anyone out there who may be a little like me. Maybe you have felt the Lord leading you to do something for a while. Maybe you are on the edge between taking that step of faith in God or remaining where it is comfortable and familiar. Maybe you look at your life and don't feel worthy or able to do the things that God has placed in your heart or called you to do. I was encouraged by God with this verse: Philippians 2:13, "For it is God who works in you both to will and do for *His* good pleasure." You don't have to worry about whether you have what it takes to do something. If God has called you to it, then He will equip you to do what He has called you toward. You only have to be willing to have courage, trust Him and take that first small step. Let God do the rest.

I.   BE STILL AND KNOW

If you spend enough time in this world, you
begin to notice that life has a certain pace to it. It
follows various rhythms and beats. It has quiet
and still moments, like when you find yourself
captivated by a sight so beautiful, so peaceful
you can't help but stand in awe of it. It also has
fast-paced almost chaotic notes to it, like when
you find yourself rushing to make it out the door
or to an event or social obligation in time. It
makes you wonder in all the movement of life,
where does God fit in? Is He something you
schedule into the first or last few minutes of the
day? Do you spend time with Him on Sundays or
Wednesday night bible studies? Maybe He's
there in that TV program or devotional you're
reading up on?

Truthfully, all of those are great ways of
connecting and growing one's faith walk and
learning more about the Father. However, if you
want to really hear from God, if you desire a
deeper more intimate relationship with God, if
you want to move past being led by fear and

doubt and start walking in confidence and authority, then you need to start making the choice to choose to Be Still and Know. Being still requires pausing, prioritizing and listening. It can't be done, while also juggling and multi-tasking 5 other events. God isn't something to be checked off on an ever-growing and never-ending agenda of life responsibilities. He needs to be chosen by you. We need to make it a point to stop and let ourself rest and be filled in the presence of the Holy One.

In Psalm 46 the Word of God describes God's character and outlines who He is to His children and those who trust in Him. He is a "very present help in trouble," "Our refuge and strength." He can make it so that even as the world around us shakes and falls, we can rest and not fear. He is described as mighty and at the very end of the psalm God makes a declaration through the Psalmist to "Be still, and know that I *am* God."

Sometimes in the busyness of life, we forget that we have a loving Father who desires to share our time with Him and wants to make Himself known to us. Growing our faith requires effort on our end. But isn't it wonderful, that the only thing God asks of us is to stop and let God be God? As we journey through this devotional together, I hope that you'll find moments outside of simply reading a devotional a day to simply sit and spend intentional time in the presence of God. Whenever, you feel that tug on your heart to turn off that TV series or open your Bible or listen to that worship song, my prayer for you is that you are obedient to that call. Moments spent with God are never a waste of time and when you really start to understand God, you will realize that there isn't anything else that should take priority over Him.

Challenge: Ask God to reveal to you moments this week, where you can make the choice to step away from a daily task and step into time with Him.

II.   OBEDIENCE OVER SACRIFICE

The choice to walk in true obedience to the Lord
will always reveal one's heart posture.
Obedience requires humility, surrender, faith and
love. In 1 Samuel 15: 10-28 King Saul is visited
and confronted by the Prophet Samuel for his
lack of obedience in following through with the
commands of God. Saul did what was right in his
own eyes and justified his actions under the guise
of saying that what he did, he did to honor the
Lord. However, Samuel corrects Saul and says in
1 Samuel 15: 22, "Has the Lord *as great* delight in
burnt offerings and sacrifices, as in obeying the
voice of the LORD? Behold, to obey is better
than sacrifice..." From the outside perspective
Saul's actions may have seemed honorable and
glorifying, but really his choice to directly
disobey the Lord's command revealed what was
inside of him -- a sinful, self-serving person
whose heart was far from the Lord.

What prevents us today from walking in
obedience to the Lord? Do we fear the outcome
of what walking in obedience might produce? Do

we not have trust and confidence that the Lord will walk with us and see us through everything He has called us to do? Is it possible that choosing obedience will require us to surrender and give up something or someone that we are unwilling to sacrifice? Whatever the reason for not walking in obedience is, one thing remains clear, it will reveal the state of your heart. Either your heart is devoted to the Lord or it's devoted to your own life. Either you have all faith and confidence in who the Lord is in your life or you walk in doubt and fear which leads to ultimately being led by an unsteady and uncertain hand. Either you choose to walk God's path and see what blessings come to you and to those around you from walking in obedience or you choose to remain as you are.

We have to make a choice. Not choosing is still a choice. It goes without saying, but obedience isn't always easy. It requires the Power of God moving through us, enabling us to do, what we cannot do in our own strength. However, the outcome will always lead to God's glory. The more you choose to follow the path that God leads you down, the easier it becomes. What once felt like climbing up a mountain will feel more like walking on a grassy path next to your best friend.

Challenge: Say "Yes" to the next thing you hear God calling you towards. Rather than being led and restrained by fear, choose to trust Him with your life.

12

III.   FROM TOP TO BOTTOM

From the very beginning of human life on Earth, God's actions have shown that He desires connection, relationship and intimacy with humanity. In the time of Adam and Eve He spent time regularly walking and communing with them in the Garden of Eden. When they broke God's one sacred command of not eating the fruit from the Tree of the Knowledge of Good and Evil, God started a centuries long pursuit of reuniting us with Him. He used prophetic words that foretold of a savior, which led to the birth of Jesus and ultimately restored our relationship with Him when Jesus made the choice to give up His life as the perfect sacrifice able to cover all of our past, present and future sins.

God pursued us. God never gave up on us. Even when our disobedience created a cavern of sin separating us from the Holy God, God still remained faithful and dedicated to us. He loves us. He wants us. He chose us to share and allow us to partake in the blessings, authority and power that comes with being His children and He

13

didn't even put the cost of that inheritance on us. He paid the cost. Like a Good Father the responsibility and consequences of our sin fell on Him. Even today that gift is still available to anyone who wants it. The gift of knowing Jesus is to choose to accept Him as our Savior and then through water baptism and the receiving of the Baptism of the Holy Spirit we can began to walk in true freedom, light and love toward all people and in all situations and circumstances. It's a power that supersedes the laws and foundations of this world, because it comes from the Creator of this world.

In Mark 15: 38 it is written that when Christ died "the veil of the temple was torn in two from top to bottom." This veil separated humanity from the presence and Spirit of the Living Holy God. There was no longer any need to have this separation. Humanity was now once again free to walk in complete unity with the Living God. The incredible part is that the veil was torn from top to bottom. We didn't restore our relationship. Our sacrifice wasn't what was needed or required to cover our sins. Instead, the Lord moved first. He tore in half the separation dividing us from Him. He closed the gap. He restored the relationship. He revealed His character and the content of His heart to us by being the One to fix what we broke by sacrificing who He loved to show us that He loves us.

Challenge: What is causing distance between you and God today? The Death and Resurrection of Jesus Christ makes it so that there is no power or authority that can separate us from the Love of God. Bring whatever sin, worry or fear you have to the feet of Jesus and let His love for you cover, heal and restore you.

IV. DOERS AND NOT HEARERS ONLY

James 2:14-26 speaks about the Biblical truth of how faith without works is dead. In James 2:26 it reads "For as the body without the spirit is dead, so faith without works is dead also." Believing in God, knowing about God, but never acting on that knowledge and belief produces nothing. It's like knowing a plant needs water and sunshine to grow but never putting it in the light or giving it the nutrients it requires. It may survive for a little while, but ultimately that plant will only die. The same can be said of our faith-walk. It is good to believe in God and know of Him, but we need to allow the Holy Spirit to convict and empower us to act and live out that faith.

James speaks about this truth in another way earlier in his book when he writes "But be doers of the word, and not hearers only, deceiving yourselves. For if anyone is a hearer of the word and not a doer, he is like a man observing his natural face in a mirror; for he observes himself, goes away, and immediately forgets what kind of man he was" (James 1:22-24). The way James compares not doing what the word says to a man who literally forgets who he is speaks volumes. If we aren't following God's Word, what are we following? If we aren't doing what is written, what are we doing? If God's word isn't what is leading us, then something else is. God is the only One who knows us, truly knows us. He knew us before we even were (Jeremiah 1:5).

If we aren't allowing His word to shape our character, thoughts and actions, then something else will. Something that doesn't align with the truth of who we are and before long, that something will become our identity, source and definition of self. We will become as James wrote: people who see ourselves, but have no idea who we really are. That's a scary place to be.

If you want to know more about yourself, you need to start with knowing about God, but you can't stop there. As you read through His Word, you need to ask the Holy Spirit to help you identify and fix the areas where your life or thoughts don't align with the Word of God. Ask Him to give you a heart that doesn't reject or harden at the reading of His word, but one that submits and pursues after His commandments.

Challenge: Ask the Holy Spirit to identify the area of your life that doesn't align with or reflect the truth of God's Word. Pray and ask the Holy Spirit to change the desires of your flesh until they align with the Word of God.

*For an explanation of the verses in this devotional that have been referenced in parenthesis but have not been directly quoted, please refer to the end section located at the back of this book titled "Explanation of Referenced Verses" starting on pg. 141.

V. LOVE THE LORD YOUR GOD

In Mark 12: 30 Jesus says the first and greatest commandment is this: "You shall love the Lord your God with all your heart, with all your soul, with all your mind, and with all your strength." As you continue reading in Mark 12: 31, He adds "And the second [commandment], is like it: You shall love your neighbor as yourself." (Words in bracket added for context.) It's interesting that loving God and loving people goes hand-in-hand. It's often said that we live in a world filled with sin and brokenness. God has already written and established a plan for a new kingdom free from all the pain, loss and sickness that is so prevalent here on Earth, but that doesn't mean there isn't very real suffering that many of us face today.

Although much of the hardship and heartache that we feel can be traced back to a person or event, we are still called to walk in love toward people. Not the tolerating kind of love either. It's the kind of love that sees a person and acts in love toward them as if they were an outward extension of ourselves. If we truly desire to show God love, we have to love people. 1 John 4:20-21 puts it this way "If someone says, 'I love God,' and hates his brother, he is a liar, for he who does not love his brother whom he has seen, how can he love God whom he has not seen? And this commandment we have from Him: that he who loves God *must* love his brother also."

In order to do step one: love God, we have to also do step two: love people. Loving people with different views, forgiving those who have hurt you, choosing to see others as Christ does is not easy. So many times, we as Christ followers are challenged to extend love to those who have shown through continuous and relentless actions against us to desire our destruction and defeat. We are called to forgive and walk in love toward those who have only ever hurt us. It's not something that we can accomplish on our own. Oftentimes, it's not a one-time, one-and-done decision. It requires us daily to give and submit that anger and hurt to the Lord and ask Him to give us a heart that can see and love others as we seek to see and love Him.

I have found that loving and forgiving people is not just for the benefit of others, but for the benefit of ourselves as well. I think we all know and have experienced the tremendous weight of being angry, hurt or at unease with someone. It affects us emotionally, mentally and physically. In some cases, our very health and energy can decline. When we ask the Lord to relieve us of that hate and unforgiveness, He lifts the burden of carrying it around off from our hearts and severs it from our minds. God knows our hearts, so when He calls us to forgive and love, it's because He knows that choosing not to do so only hurts ourselves. God desires for us to have true freedom, so the commandments that He gives us should be viewed with that truth in mind. They aren't burdensome rules that must be obeyed simply to be obeyed. They are loving commandments given, so that we can truly have life and have it more abundantly.

Challenge: Is there someone you need to forgive whose actions have caused you pain? Ask the Lord to search your heart and make known to you the areas or people where the

love of God and/or the love of people is not prevalent in your life.

VI.   THE LORD IS

In a world where we often feel as though we have to be quick to respond, quick to act, quick to defend, God offers us a counter perspective through the psalmist David. In Psalm 18 David reveals pieces of God's character by describing who the Lord is by *how* He delivered him from all of His enemies. David confidently proclaims that the Lord is his strength, his rock, his fortress, his deliverer, his shield, and the horn of his salvation. The Lord is described as someone worthy to be praised and someone in whom he can trust. The Lord is a support and light. These are just a few of the attributes of the Lord which David writes about in the psalm.

How would we go through life if we also knew the Lord by all of these attributes? Would we still fear an unknown outcome, person or threat? Would we continue to go through life feeling as though we need to have a wall around our hearts and a mask over our face to protect from possible rejection or abandonment? Throughout the Bible, the Lord takes the time to describe His heart and His character to us, so that we as His children can know with all confidence what we have in Him. We don't need to be strong in every circumstance, because God's strength rests on us. We don't have to be unattainably perfect, because God knows and anticipated our shortcomings and offered His Son's life as an alternative to the consequences of sin. We don't have to fear the dark and all that lies within it, because the light of the Lord can and will not be overcome.

Next time you find yourself in a situation you don't want to be in or facing a problem that feels too big to handle, remember who your God is. Remember that His might has no limit. Remember that there is no problem, that His wisdom and understanding cannot answer. Remember He is a Good Father who desires to reveal Himself mighty to you.

Challenge: Find a characteristic of God in the Bible. Write it down, speak it out, commit it to memory and when the time comes declare it over yourself, over your loved ones or over your situation. The same God who delivered David is the same God who calls you His own.

VII.   BEGINNING OF WISDOM

In today's society there are many examples of knowledge, wisdom and understanding. We feel knowledgeable when we learn a new skill or acquire a new title. We feel wise when the application of our hard work produces fruit or a positive outcome. Our understanding feels heightened when we have an experience that affects and changes us. While these things can be good in our lives, they can also be used as alternatives for true wisdom, knowledge and understanding.

Proverbs 9: 10 reads "The fear of the Lord *is* the beginning of wisdom, and the knowledge of the Holy One *is* understanding." How we grow our knowledge, wisdom and understanding matters. If it is pulled from any source outside of God, it may provide temporary comfort, relief and a sense of accomplishment, but over time that will fail and fade. If we really want to be wise, knowledgeable and have understanding of people and the workings of this world, we have to start with having reverence and honor for the things of God. We need to familiarize ourselves with His statutes. We have to meditate on the meaning of His Word. We have to invite the Holy Spirit to reveal to us, that which we cannot understand on our own.

The more we grow closer to God, the more we understand people. The more we understand people, the more we begin to see the patterns of this world. The more we identify those patterns, the more we are able to recognize the truth from the lies, the imitations from the authentic, the things that free us from the things that bind us up more. God gave us the first step. We have to start with honoring and approaching Him with a humbled heart.

Challenge: Take inventory of your life and your thoughts. Where does the source of your wisdom, understanding and knowledge lie? Does its source come from God or from something else entirely? Compare the truths you live by with what is written in God's Word. If they don't line up, reevaluate and submit what doesn't belong to the Lord.

VIII.   GOD IS LOVE

God loves us. It's a phrase many of us have heard at one point in our lives. For some, that phrase is a source of comfort and truth. For others, it is accompanied with uncertainty and questions around the authenticity of that statement. Some have heard it used so often, that the true meaning of those words has lost the once powerful effect they had on their overall well-being. Today I hope to remind and reveal to you why the words "God Loves Us" have become such a commonly used part of Christian vocabulary.

In 1 John 4: 8, John makes the powerful proclamation that "God is love." God is love. 3 simple words that hold so much meaning and reveal the very essence of who God is, why He behaves the way He does and how He can continuously pursue after, choose and desire us, even when we do everything in our power to push Him away. To understand that God is love, we have to first understand that God's love is not to be compared with human love. Human love can be temporary, conditional, and flawed.

God's love is not like that. His love is faithful, even when we are not faithful (2 Timothy 2:13). His love is merciful and full of grace (Romans 5:8). His love is given with the intent to free and uplift us (John 8:32). His love isn't dependent on our own goodness or our own ability to be "enough." His love makes us enough. His love validates us. If there is one thing you can rely on to stay consistent and never change or be taken away, it's this: God Loves You. He always has, He does today, and He always will.

Challenge: Think of a time when you received something you didn't deserve or a time when you didn't receive a negative consequence that you deserved. Those are examples of grace and mercy. God is constantly pouring out His grace and mercy on us, but we don't always recognize the multiple ways that He does. Next time you find yourself on the receiving end of His goodness, don't just chock it up to luck or coincidence. Instead, give credit where credit is due. Recognize and thank the Lord for His goodness in your life.

IX.   WORSHIP IN SPIRIT AND TRUTH

We are called to worship. Every created thing
has within itself the ability to honor, uplift and
worship God. When Jesus made His descent
down the Mount of Olives on a colt near the end
of His time on Earth, Jesus so famously said to
the pharisees who rebuked his disciples for
worshipping Him, "I tell you that if these [the
multitude of his disciples] should keep silent, the
stones would immediately cry out (words added
for context)" (Luke 19: 40). Even stones on the
ground could cry out and worship the Living
God if given the command. But what is worship?

Is worship the clapping of hands in time with the
drummer, choir or worship leaders? Does true
worship only occur when that exact song hits at
that exact moment when you need it or really
want it to? Can only those born with a voice and
the ability to produce sound through their vocal
cords worship the almighty God? True worship,
the kind of worship that is in spirit and truth has
to be more than what we can accomplish on our
own. It requires the extra element of God's Spirit

31

and Truth moving through, over and around us to create the kind of authentic worship that would be pleasing to the Lord and glorify His holiness.

Jesus once met a woman at a well in the beginning of His ministry and He told her "But the hour is coming, and now is, when the true worshippers will worship the Father in spirit and truth; for the Father is seeking such to worship Him. God *is* Spirit, and those who worship Him must worship in spirit and truth" (John 4: 23-24). This means that true worship isn't limited to a place, such as a temple or a church building. Since it requires the presence of spirit in order for it to be true worship, it's safe to say that true worship is less about the song that we sing, how pretty our voice sounds or how high we raise our hands and it is more about connecting with God. It is about getting to the place where we become aware of His presence, His holiness, His reverence and we make the choice to magnify, exalt and glorify Him, because He is God and deserves nothing less.

Because of the death and resurrection of Jesus Christ we are no longer limited to worship God at the temple, located only inside the Holy City of Jerusalem. We have full access to Him at all times and in all circumstances and situations. Worshipping in spirit and truth isn't reliant upon our emotions either. It doesn't require us to feel like everything is "all good now" before we can worship Him. Just as it doesn't only occur when you hit rock bottom and suddenly look up and realize God was there with you all along.

We worship God for who He is and not for how we feel, who we are or what our lives look like now. That isn't to say that we don't still receive from Him when we choose to worship in a God-centered, not us-centered manner. In Isaiah 61: 3 Isaiah speaks about how God can give us "the garment of praise for the spirit of heaviness." When we praise God, there are things that happen in the spirit that can affect us in the natural (physical world). The primary focus of worshipping should be to honor and magnify the Lord, but that doesn't mean that we don't still benefit from being in His presence and choosing to honor Him regardless of what our lives look like in that moment or how we feel.

Challenge: It isn't always easy to worship God in the middle of trials and hardships. It truly does require us to take our eyes off of ourselves and place them on our Father. Make the choice to find time to worship the Lord. Declare His goodness, honor him by sacrificing your time in exchange for His glory and be intentional about lifting His name higher than everything else.

X.   GUARD YOUR HEART AND EYES

When we think of the word "guard" we directly associate it with the word "protect." After all, if you are guarding something, then that must mean that there is something that wants to steal, destroy or harm it. In Philippians 4: 6-7 Paul cautions us to "be anxious for nothing, but in everything by prayer and supplication, with thanksgiving, let your requests be made known to God; and the peace of God, which surpasses all understanding, will guard your hearts and minds through Christ Jesus." Paul knew that our peace and sense of stability would be under attack from outside forces. Maybe it's those bills piling up, or that family member/friend going through it or one of the many other challenges that we face in this life coming at us again from all angles seeking to destroy what little peace and joy we have found.

It's all but a guarantee, that in this life something will happen to you or around you that is jarring and dysregulating. That's why we must be on guard. We need to be so trained, so diligent, that when these life events occur and seek to knock us off our footing, our first response isn't to panic and spiral. Instead, we remember and call on the name of our God, who is the only One mighty and able us to deliver us through any and all trials. That deliverance may not always look the way we want it to though. Sometimes, there are lessons we only learn after we have walked through the trial. Sometimes, there are pieces of our character that only form after we experience the hardship. Sometimes, we can only confidently declare God as mighty, a healer, a provider and our defender only after we have witnessed Him be mighty, heal, provide and defend us in our own lives.

Matthew 6: 22-23 reads "The lamp of the body is the eye. If therefore your eye is good, your whole body will be full of light. But if your eye is bad, your whole body will be full of darkness." What we see, what we allow to have access to us, who we choose to be around and what we do, does have an effect on our overall well-being. There are some situations that are out of our control. We can't control who our co-workers are, who are family is, or what music our neighbors choose to play, but there are things that are well within our limits to control. It's important that we take account of what we are allowing to enter and affect us.

Our environment influences the way we think, how we act, and what we believe. If the only influences around you work to counter or disagree with the truth of God's Word, how long will it be before you begin to doubt who God says He is? Even without meaning to, if left unchecked and unguarded the influences of this world can begin to change and form our idea of truth and who we know God to be. We can't be passive. We must guard our hearts and eyes. Make no mistake there is a fight for what/who will control your heart and if you aren't defending the truth of God's word, then the truth will be stolen from you.

Challenge: When we are initially faced with a problem or situation that is not in alignment with who we are called to be as God's children, there is a tugging on our hearts from the Holy Spirit. However, over time if we

ignore or act in our own interest, that voice, that tug can become quieter and quieter. When was the last time you felt the Spirit of God telling you "no" or pulling you away from something? Did you listen and walk away?

XI. HARDEN NOT YOUR HEART

God could force obedience. He could force
worship. He could force love, but then would it
really be obedience, worship or love? Perhaps
one of the greatest gifts God has given us is the
gift of choice. Also known as, the gift of free
will. God knew when He designed the world and
its inhabitants with this gift, that there would be
those who would choose not to choose Him. He
even knew that there would be those who chose
to make it their life mission to disagree, destroy
and redefine everything He is and all He desires
for us to have. However, He still gave us the gift
of choice.

There is a calling over each of our lives. There is
an intentional purpose that God has given all of
His creation. We were not accidently thrown
together haphazardly with no real concern for
what the final product would look like. Psalms
139: 13-14 says "For you formed my inward
parts; You covered me in my mother's womb. I
will praise You, for I am fearfully and
wonderfully made; marvelous are Your works,

and that my soul knows well." You may have felt
or even been told that you don't matter or that
you are replaceable or that the world would go
on spinning without you. However, that couldn't
be further from the truth. Not only do you matter,
but you are important and wonderful in the sight
of the One who created you. God took the time to
create you. He decided that you, yes you, were so
worth it, that He dedicated the works of His
hands to craft, create and give life to you.

We have to know that our being here at this time,
with the life we have been given, isn't a
coincidence or accidental. There is something
uniquely special in each of us that God brought
to life on this Earth, when He created us. He
didn't just create us and then walk away like an
absentee parent. He calls to us. To truly
understand our purpose, our calling on this Earth
we have to be in relationship with Christ.
Hebrews 3: 14-15 declares "For we have become
partakers of Christ if we hold the beginning of
our confidence steadfast to the end, while it is
said: Today, if you will hear His voice, do not
harden your hearts as in the rebellion."

There is a choice each of us must make at some point in our lives. We don't know how much time we each have to make it. God calls to each of us to find and establish ourselves in Him. His voice beckons us to receive and accept His Son as our savior. He desires to pour out the gift of the Holy Spirit over us, so that in all things we have a perfect guide, teacher, counselor, and helper to help us walk through and face each season of our lives (John 16: 13 & John 14: 16). He has in no way left us alone and He never will (Matthew 28: 20). But accepting and choosing Him is our choice. He won't force us. What choice will you make? What choice have you made?

Challenge: God doesn't only call to us once. He calls for us to receive salvation. He calls for us to walk away from the things that will only produce death and destruction in our lives. He calls for us to walk in the fullness of grace, mercy and forgiveness toward ourselves and others. He calls us to trust Him with our lives and our purposes and to walk in obedience with the gifts that He has placed in

us, surrendering them all back to Him. How is
God calling you today? How will you answer?

XII.   THAT MAN SHOULD BE ALONE

When God created Adam, one of the first things
He said was "*It is* not good that man should be
alone; I will make him a helper comparable to
him." (Genesis 2:18). If the Lord of all creation
realized that people need people, why do we find
ourselves believing and living the lie that we
have to do everything "all on our own" or "I
can't trust anyone, but myself" or "I'm just not a
people person," when we were quite literally
created with the intention of going through life
with the help of others. This mindset that has
become so common in our culture. However, it is
actually a lie of deception made by the enemy to
go against our original Godly design.

In Ecclesiastes 4: 9-10 it says "Two are better
than one, because they have a good reward for
their labor. For if they fall, one will lift up his
companion. But woe to him *who is* alone when
he falls, for *he* has no one to help him up." It's
true that if you set it in your mind to complete a
task, you could probably get it done by yourself.
However, how much extra time would it take?
How much more effort would be required of you

if you go at it all alone? How much greater is the chance that you risk injury to yourself, an injury that could've been avoided if you had the extra hand? You might be reading this and thinking to yourself. "I'd love to have the extra help, but there's no one to help me." To that I say two things:

1) Have you actually made the attempt to verbalize to another person that you need or would like help? You may think it's obvious when people need help, but remember that people aren't mind readers. Sometimes you need to be direct and make the need or want known. The situation doesn't always have to be a dire situation for you to ask for help. You are allowed to ask for help for something that is easy and totally doable on your own, but you have to make sure you actually verbalize it.

2) If you truly have no one to ask, because maybe you moved to a new area or the friend or family relationship dynamics around you has changed, then ask God to send someone. Pray and ask God to send people who will encourage, help and challenge you for the better. He's already proven

in His word that He sees the need for us to have other people in our lives, so why would a Good Father withhold a good thing from His children (Matthew 7:9-11)?

There exist within this world deceptions that the enemy has been planting into the foundations of truth. They seem small and harmless. After all, what's wrong with trying to be "independent and doing everything on your own." At first, maybe nothing. However, over time that mindset can turn into something truly damaging.

What happens when you find yourself in true need of someone's help, but you have set this persona/identity around yourself that you are self-confident, self-sufficient, and always have to be the "strong one?" Will you really allow yourself to be vulnerable in that moment and reach out to someone for help? Or will you hide, keeping your pain and issues to yourself as the damage they do continues to grow and you are left far more broken and emotionally and mentally-impaired; all because you tried to do on your own what you were never meant to do on your own? Don't believe the lie. Don't fall for the deception. It's okay that we all need help. You were literally created to not be alone, so don't go through life alone.

Challenge: The next time you have a task that you want to accomplish or you feel emotionally or mentally distraught over something big or small, invite a trusted individual into that moment with you. Don't go at it alone. Go through it with someone.

XIII.   PRODUCTION OF CHARACTER

I think it's safe to say that no one wants to go through hardships. I can't say I've ever met anyone that earnestly searches for trials and sufferings to come their way. On the other hand, I also can't say that I've ever met someone who hasn't gone through hardships, trials or sufferings. We live in a world of brokenness and sin and with that comes loss, health concerns, financial difficulties, mental and emotional distress and so many other countless examples of how being alive on this Earth is not easy. God already has a plan to rid the world of all of these things, but in the meantime, He didn't leave us to face and battle our sufferings alone with no help or hope.

In Romans 5:1-5 Paul writes about the gift and blessings that comes with going through hardships with Jesus. Verse 3-4 reads "And not only *that*, but we also glory in tribulations, knowing that tribulations produces perseverance; and perseverance, character; and character, hope." When you experience a loss outside of Jesus without the power of the Holy Spirit living and reviving you daily, it's easy to think thoughts like: "I'm just built to have a hard life," "this is just how it's always going to be" or "everyone else just has it easier than me". These thoughts when left unchecked can began to develop a warped image of life, God and people. It can make it harder to see past or see anything other than what is going wrong in our lives. Before long, even the blessings and good moments will only be seen through the lens of negativity and pessimism.

There's a popular saying that "what doesn't kill me makes me stronger." I think it's important to point out that not all trials produce a stronger, more resilient character. Actually, it's very common for them to produce quite the opposite. They can leave you feeling envious or bitter toward the perceived happiness and blessings of others. You can be left feeling alone and abandoned like no one cares or sees you. You can even begin to value yourself less and develop habits that numb your mind and emotions and leave you completely unable to function on a day-to-day basis without the need of an additional substance to get through a task that you once got through with such ease.

Only trials that we go through with Jesus produce the kind of firm foundation that we need to be able to face the storms of life and not find ourselves feeling and believing that we are completely destroyed or broken beyond repair (Matthew 7: 24-27). When you go through a tribulation with Jesus and with the power of the Holy Spirit, you find yourself referring back to His word and speaking it over yourself. Words like "casting all your care upon Him, for He cares for you" (1 Peter 5: 7) or "Yea, though I walk through the valley of the shadow of death, I will fear no evil; for You *are* with me; Your rod and Your staff, they comfort me" to name a few (Psalms 23: 4).

Before long, you start walking through that trial with the unwavering belief that the Lord will you see you through this. This perseverance creates a stronger character. The type of character that now knows that you can make it through the difficulties of life and not crumble. The kind of character that learns how to pray, declare and believe in the promises of God, because you have seen them in and over your life. The kind of character that the next time you face a trial or tribulation, you walk into it knowing that God walks with you. The kind of character that is confident that He protects and covers you and that He will see you through any and all situations. That type of character produces a hope, that *even* when things look like they are at their worst and *even* when you don't have the strength or ability to solve, heal, or fix the problem on your own, you know that there is a God that loves you who can. Trials and tribulations will produce character, but which character they will produce depends on who/what you put your faith in. Put your faith in Jesus. Walk through it with Jesus.

Challenge: Don't wait for the trial or tribulation to occur to have your verse battle ready. Find a promise of God to speak over yourself now. In moments of suffering, it can be hard to encourage yourself to go to God's word. Have your verse at the ready now and pray to the Lord to bring it to your

remembrance for when you face that next mountain or find yourself in that valley.

XIV.   PLANTED BY THE WATER

We live in a time when knowledge abounds, and
we have instant access to all kinds of information
at the touch of our fingers. With one quick
Google search, we can quickly identify different
species of plants. By watching a video online, we
can see with our very own eyes the wonders and
atrocities occurring on the other side of the
world. As our understanding and knowledge of
the world grows, some have taken it upon
themselves to question where and if God fits into
all of this. After all, with so much information at
our ready, do we *really* still need the Lord?

I'm here to say that it is possible to grow in
knowledge *and* also grow further and further
away from the truth. There is a self-assured, self-
validated mindset and belief that can grow with
not bringing God into our learning or including
Him in our discoveries. Not everything in this
world is as it seems.

Not every newfound "truth" is actually truthful.
The Bible puts it this way "Cursed *is* the man

who trusts in man and makes flesh his strength, whose heart departs from the LORD" (Jeremiah 17: 5). In other words when you decide it upon yourself to trust in the knowledge of man over the word of God, you set yourself up for destruction. Be aware, it's not always a conscious decision. Sometimes you make the choice and you don't even realize you are making the choice. Sometimes we choose to believe that praying to God can't heal us, so we seek out alternative methods. Other times we believe that true inner peace can only be found deep within the constructs of nature and forget what Jesus promised about peace in the first place (John 14: 27). Please don't misunderstand. Nature and medicine aren't bad. However, anything that we put in place of God or place before Him is bad.

The Bible actually writes the gameplan for how to be successful, thrive and secure in all seasons using the metaphor of a tree. Psalms 1: 2-3 writes "But his delight *is* in the law of the LORD, and in His law he meditates day and night. He shall be like a tree planted by the rivers of water, that brings forth its fruit in its season, whose leaf also shall not wither; and whatever he does shall prosper." Jeremiah 17:7 adds "Blessed *is* the man who trusts in the LORD, and whose hope is the LORD. For he shall be like a tree planted by the waters, which spreads out its roots by the river, and will not fear when heat comes; but its leaf will be green, and will not be anxious in the year of drought, nor will cease from yielding fruit."

When you think about a tree and what it needs to be nourished and survive, you might immediately imagine that it needs water and that the soil/place it's planted needs to be conducive to sustaining life. For example, if you place a tree on a plastic tarp, it might survive for a little while, but it's safe to say it won't last forever. The same can be said of people. What we believe and who/what we place our trust in will determine if and how we grow. In both Jeremiah and in the Psalms, the authors speak of the importance of the Biblical truth of trusting, hoping, and spending time seeking to understand God's word by meditating on it day and night. We live in a world where we are constantly presented with alternatives and multiple paths to get what we really want. However, having faith and trust in God, Jesus and the Holy Spirit is the only way forward that will forever remain constantly secure and allow us to grow and flourish everlastingly (Matthew 7: 13-14 & John 14: 10).

Challenge: Prioritizing and choosing to have faith in God requires effort on our end. It isn't passive. It involves active determination to stand solely and firmly on the Word of God. What is something you are seeking or wanting to see happen or change in your life? Go to the Lord, meditate on His word, spend time in prayer and worship with Him. James 4:8 says "Draw near to God and He will draw near to you." God has and is your answer. Get into communion with Him and see how He reveals the truth to you.

XV.   70 X 7

When Jesus came into the picture, He took the laws of this world and flipped them upside down. He introduced a new, rearranged way of living that put love first before our own self-gratification. When his disciple Peter asked Him if seven times was enough when it comes to forgiving a brother who has wronged you, Jesus took the revenge motivated law of "an eye for an eye" and in its place He told His disciple "I do not say to you, up to seven times, but up to seventy times seven" (Matthew 18:22). This statement might not seem like much, but it was revolutionary and counter-cultural according to the laws of that time.

Forgiving someone one time already requires a lot on our end, especially when you consider the hurt, betrayal and loss of trust that comes with needing to be forgiven. Forgiving them seven times is surely a generous amount, because anything past that would just be "foolish." However, making the choice to forgive someone from your heart 70 x 7 times was unheard of. The kind of forgiveness Jesus was referring to wasn't just some surface level kind of verbal agreement either. It required really going to the depth of your heart and forgiving them.

Following these words, Jesus used Matthew 18:23-35 to tell the parable of a servant who had a great debt, went to his master and because of the compassion of his master, all of his debt was forgiven. However, instead of being filled with mercy and compassion, that servant instead goes to a second servant who owes him a much smaller amount than what the first servant owed. He threatened and threw the man into prison until he could repay what he owed the first servant, who was originally forgiven of his debt. When word gets around to the master who had forgiven the first servant all of his debt, the master becomes exceedingly angry and delivers him to those who would make him pay all that was originally due to the master.

This parable is reflective of how, as God's children, we have been forgiven a great debt. When Jesus died, He forgave the world of all of its sins and made it possible for us to go to Him to receive forgiveness for any present or future sins that we might commit. He forgave us of all our sins and didn't require anything on our part to cover the cost. He allowed Himself to be beaten, tortured, mocked and eventually killed, so that we wouldn't have to bear the burden and consequences of our own sinful nature and actions. He did all of this knowing that not everyone would believe or accept this great gift of love. In other words, He had no guarantee that all of humanity would accept His sacrifice for what it was, a gift and display of His love for all of creation. Yet, He still did it simply so that we would have the option of forgiveness on the table. Jesus' love through action gives us a way out if we chose to accept it.

This parable imparts the importance of not just being on the receiving end of mercy, but also extending and giving out mercy. It reveals the condition of one's heart. Do you go through life with a heart only counting and recording all the things that are owed to you or do you choose to see people through the same lens of grace and mercy that was bestowed upon you?

Challenge: How can you extend mercy, grace and/or forgiveness to those around you today? Really look around. There are countless opportunities to show kindness to others if we slow down and take a moment to notice.

XVI.   SEARCH ME, O GOD AND KNOW

"Search me, O God, and know my heart; try me,
and know my anxieties; and see if *there is any*
wicked way in me, and lead me in the way
everlasting" (Psalms 139: 23-24). SEARCH me,
TRY me, SEE, and LEAD me. SEARCH me:
look and find the depth of my heart. TRY me:
put me to the test, reveal who I am, when push
comes to shove. SEE: make the final verdict on
any evilness within me. LEAD me: guide and
show me a better path, Your path.

When we first make the choice to accept Jesus as
our Lord and Savior, we receive the gift of
salvation. As we grow in our relationship with
Him, through the workings of the Holy Spirit
within us He begins the lifelong process of
correcting, removing and growing us so that our
heart, mind and actions reflect His. This is called
sanctification (Hebrews 10: 14, Hebrews 13: 12 &
John 17: 17). Sanctification is an ongoing process,
through one's faith walk, because we
continuously need the grace and mercy of God to
pursue a life with Jesus.

Far too often Christians, after receiving salvation, will place the uncalled-for pressure of trying to be perfect on themselves, when what they are really attempting to pursue is sanctification. They are trying to become better, but may get that confused with the idea of believing that it means they can never make any mistakes or ever show weakness, which is a burden that the Lord never desired to place on us. Instead, He gave us His Spirit, the Holy Spirit, the great counselor and comforter, to guide, correct and convict us in our pursuit of having a better, closer relationship with the Lord, Jesus (John 16: 13 & John 14: 16).

Psalms 139: 23-24 is an excellent example of David's prayer for sanctification. He's not self-justifying himself or proclaiming himself to be without fault. Instead, He's inviting the Lord into his life and asking Him to be the judge of who he is and help him make right within him what is not. It's a beautiful and powerful prayer, that if done from a place of surrender and the desire to grow closer to the Lord, can lead to a new depth in our relationship and faith walk with God.

Challenge: We are not perfect. Self-attained perfection was never meant to be the goal, so we shouldn't place that burden on ourselves. Is there an area where you have found yourself struggling to change? Is there an area of your life that you aren't proud of, but you keep hitting the same wall when it comes to overcoming it? Don't go at it alone. Invite the Lord into it with you. Don't hide what doesn't look right from Him. Instead, pray the prayer of sanctification in Psalms 139:23-24. Be continuous about bringing it to the Lord, no matter how many times it takes. Just like it takes a while before an action becomes a habit we're not proud of, sometimes it takes a while before a habit we're not proud of becomes broken.

XVII.   AS FOR ME

When the Holy Spirit first gave me the words
"As for me," I immediately thought of the verse
in Joshua 24:15, where Joshua boldly declares
that he and his house will serve the Lord.
However, as I did my research and looked into it,
the phrase "As for me" appears multiple times
within the Bible. "As for me, I will call upon
God, and the Lord shall save me" (Psalms 55:16).
"As for me, You uphold me in my integrity, and
set me before Your face forever" (Psalms 41:12).
"But as for me, I trust in You, O LORD; I say,
"You are my God" (Psalms 31:14). These are just
a few of the many "As for me" verses in the
Bible.

The Word of the Lord is filled with these
statements of beliefs. For one reason or another,
these people make the definitive declaration to
openly proclaim where they stand and what/who
they believe in. There comes a time when we as
believers will have to make the same choice. In
fact, it's more accurate to say that there will
come many moments in our lives when we have

to decide where we stand. Receiving water baptism is a public declaration to the world that you have decided to follow Jesus. Daniel's three friends Hananiah, Mishael and Azariah (also known as Shadrach, Meshach and Abed-Nego) declared that they would not bow to worship the golden image set up by Nebuchadnezzar, even knowing that they faced the risk of being delivered into the fiery furnace (Daniel 3: 12-18). Later Daniel purposed in his heart, after the king decreed that no one could petition any god or man except for him for the length of thirty days, to sit in front of an open window to pray and make supplications to the Living God. This was a decision that resulted in Him being found guilty of a crime the penalty of which was to be thrown into the lion's den (Daniel 6: 10-12).

Daniel could have closed his door and prayed in secret. He could have kept worshipping and honoring God in reverence in a way that no one would know about, which could have allowed him to avoid persecution altogether. However, he decided long ago that his God, the One true Living God wasn't a secret to be kept away, hidden or ashamed of. The Lord had not denied, abandoned or rejected him, so he wasn't going to do the same. Standing for the Lord requires courage and conviction. Deciding in one's heart to choose Jesus above and before all else involves faith.

Jesus said "Therefore whoever confesses Me before men, him I will also confess before My Father who is in heaven" (Matthew 10: 32), but He also cautions "But whoever denies Me before men, him I will also deny before My Father who is in heaven" (Matthew 10: 33). Just as there is a reward to choosing Jesus, there is also a cost to denying Him. It's a decision we each have to make for ourselves. Maybe you've made the choice to deny Him in the past. Please know that there is grace that can cover even that choice, if we go to Him, repent and make the choice to choose Him today.

Challenge: Is there something preventing you from going all in with God? What is the stumbling block in your path that is stopping you from taking that next step of faith or obedience that the Lord is calling you to in

your relationship with Him? Maybe it's fear. Maybe you worry about how you will be perceived. Maybe it's the possible rejection of those in your life that is hindering you. Whatever the cause, ask yourself are you willing to pay the cost of rejecting God? Do those reasons outweigh the importance of having a relationship with Him?

XVIII.   MEANT IT FOR GOOD

If there was ever person in the Bible who had
every reason to hold a grudge, Joseph would fit
that description. Joseph was a son favored by his
father and sold into slavery by his brothers,
because of the prophetic nature of his dreams.
After being sold into slavery, his master's wife
became infatuated with him and when Joseph
refused her advances, she lied about him and had
him thrown into prison. While in prison, Joseph
interpreted the other prisoners' dreams. He asked
only that one of the prisoners remember him and
make mention of him to Pharaoh, only to be
forgotten by that same man. It wasn't until years
later that his name was remembered and Joseph
was released from prison after being brought in
before Pharaoh to interpret his dreams (Genesis
37 - Genesis 41: 1-41).

All of this would be enough to make even the
most hopeful person bitter and doubtful of the
plan over their life. However, at the end of
Joseph's story we find him face-to-face with the
same brothers whose actions orchestrated the

series of misfortunes and tragedies that befell him. After testing them to see whether their hearts had changed or not, he discovered that they were repentant (Genesis 42 – Genesis 45). He then revealed himself to his brothers and made this powerful statement: "But as for you, you meant evil against me; *but* God meant it for good, in order to bring it about as *it is* this day, to save many people alive" (Genesis 50: 20).

It isn't always possible or easy to understand why certain things happen in our lives. In fact, most of the time, it's only in hindsight that we *really* gain clarity. Joseph was able to see, at the end of everything, how God's purpose and plan had not departed from his life. He was able to understand how God can even use the misfortune in our lives to bless others. It isn't an easy perspective to have. Walking with Jesus does involve accepting that we can't escape all hardships and sufferings. It also calls us to love those who wish and do us harm. In Matthew 5: 44-45 Jesus says this "But I say to you, love your enemies, bless those who curse you, do good to those who hate you, and pray for those who spitefully use you and persecute you, that you may be sons of your Father in heaven; for He makes His sun to rise on the evil and on the good, and sends rain on the just and on the unjust."

I don't know what you are facing today. I don't know what aches your heart or the ways that you have been hurt. My prayer for you is that as you walk through what you walk through, you do it with Jesus and that through all of it, He reminds you that the plan and purpose over your life remains and that you know that God is able to turn what is meant for evil and make it good.

Challenge: Read the story of Joseph. It's lengthy, but it's a great read. There are so many revelations that can be pulled from his story and you may even find that some of what he goes through aligns with how you feel or what you have experienced. God uses the testimonies of people in the Bible to teach and show us that our situations are not unique only to us and just as God was present for Joseph, He is also present for you.

XIX.   CAST THE FIRST STONE

Something happens to us the longer we are in a relationship with Jesus. As we grow closer to Him, we become more aware of our own shortcomings, both past and present. We also become aware of the ways in which the lives of the people around us do or don't match what is written in His word. In other words, we become sensitive to sin and anything that works in opposition of God. On the one hand, being aware of our shortcomings can allow us to identify the areas we need to change and present them to our Savior in humility, which allows Him to begin to work on our hearts and minds to make us more like Him (Psalms 51: 10 & Romans 12: 2). On the other hand, if we are not led by a humbled heart, we can begin to move in judgement and condemnation of others rather than in grace, mercy, forgiveness and love.

In John 8: 1-12 Jesus finds himself confronted by the Pharisees and scribes. He is asked how a woman found in the act of adultery should be punished. Jesus ignores them and begins writing with His finger on the ground. However, after being asked continuously if the woman should be stoned, according to the Law of Moses, He responds by saying "He who is without sin among you, let him throw a stone at her first" (John 8: 7). As you read further in that passage an interesting description of the events that follow is made. It says "Then those who heard *it*, being convicted by *their* conscience, went out one by one, beginning with the oldest *even* to the last" (John 8: 9).

Beginning with the oldest *even* to the last. The ones who had lived the most life found themselves amongst the first to leave. I think a comparison can be made between those who were older in their life to those who are older in their faith walk. As we learn more about God and His holiness and become more aware of the brokenness that exists in this world, we can't allow our hearts to become numb to others that are new to their faith *or* those who have yet to get to know the gift of having a relationship with God through Jesus. We don't get to put on the title of judge, jury and executioner.

Instead, we should be the ones whose hearts are more tender to others. We should be overcome with joy for the limitless amounts of grace, mercy and forgiveness that God has poured out on us in our lives. We should be grateful for the many ways He covered us, when we made conscious and unconscious choices that didn't align with the Holiness of God. We should be praying that God extends the same grace and mercy given to us to those that don't know Him yet. We should be acutely aware of the fact that we have no right to cast the first stone.

Challenge: We are all in need of our Savior Jesus Christ. When Jesus died, it wasn't just for those who had their lives together. In fact, His word makes it abundantly clear that "all have sinned and fall short of the glory of God" (Romans 3:23). Next time you find yourself faced with an opportunity to judge another, remember that Jesus died for that person, just as much as He died for you. If Jesus (the only worthy one) didn't cast the first stone, then who are we to?

XX. PRAY WITHOUT CEASING

1 Thessalonians 5:17 says "pray without ceasing." This verse is sandwiched in some other commandments for what aligns with the will of God in Christ Jesus. However, I want to focus on the words "pray without ceasing." To do something without ceasing means to do something without stopping. To pray means to step away and spend time with God in conversation. This conversation could be to edify or magnify, to repent, or to supplicate. The purpose and topics found and discussed in prayer are too limitless for me to list. That said, there is an element of relationship to prayer.

When you think of relationships with people, whether it is a family member, a friend, or a colleague, there is an aspect of time spent together that must be present in order for that relationship to grow. If you never talk or hangout, how can you become close? How can you get to know that individual? How can a bond be formed? The same can be said of having a relationship with God. If we don't spend time

77

with God, in prayer, in worship, in the reading of His Word, how could our relationship strengthen and last through the toughest of trials to the greatest of blessings?

When I think of "pray without ceasing," I think of being intentional about spending time with God. It's about making the commitment to be honest and pour out the content of your heart to Him. It's choosing to humble your heart and allow His Word to take root, grow and produce fruit in your life. Our prayer life can't be a side thought, or an optional part of our faith walk. It needs to be prioritized daily. I have never grown so much, as when I started to prioritize prayer in my life. We have to spend time with God in all of the seasons of our lives. We need to get to know God, when everything in our lives is joy-filled and flourishing just as much as we also need to spend time with Him, when it seems like everything we know and have confidence in is falling apart around us.

Once we know that God is with us through all of our life events, we'll get to know Him not just as our Savior, but also as our friend. A friend who's

there when we feel weak and alone (Isaiah 41: 10).
A friend whose heart is for us (Ephesians 2: 4). A
friend who feels joy just getting to spend time
with us (Psalms 145: 15-19). A friend who is
faithful even when we are not (2 Timothy 2: 13).
What a blessing it is to know the creator of the
universe as our friend.

**Challenge: God calls to us constantly
(Revelation 3:20). Next time you feel the Lord
tugging at your heart or pulling on your mind
to come spend time with Him, do it. Step away
from whatever is going on and spend time
with Him. Turn off that TV show or movie,
reschedule that event, take the time and just
be with the Lord. You won't regret it.**

XXI.   NOT BY MIGHT, NOR BY POWER

We've all found ourselves in a position where we've been face-to-face with what seems like an incomprehensibly large task. Maybe we tried to go at it all on our own. Maybe we've tried to fix the problem, stop the argument or accomplish the task all by our own ability. In Zechariah 4:6, the Lord gives a powerful word to Zerubbabel in which He says "Not by might nor by power, but by My Spirit." Further along in verses 7-9 the Lord says that even a great mountain will become a plain before Zerubbabel. He then says that what Zerubbabel started, he will finish in regard to laying the foundation of the temple.

There were things that the Lord called Zerubbabel to complete, but those things were not small to say the least. You could say that Zerubbabel was facing a mountain, and he was standing at its base. One could imagine the thoughts going through his mind knowing what he was called to accomplish. He probably felt overwhelmed and unqualified for the task. Perhaps you can relate. You may have had a dream, vision or a plan that seems too big to finish or too improvable to ever come to pass or be true. I'm here to remind you that what might be too much in our own power, ability or might is never too much for God's Spirit. In fact, if what you face is something the Lord has called you toward, then you can rest knowing that His Spirit will get you there.

In Zechariah 4:10 the following question is posed "For who has despised the day of small things?" Often times when we are faced with something bigger than us, we find ourselves very aware of where we are at that moment. Think of Moses. He was called to set God's people free, but at that moment he was hiding out in Midian (Exodus 2:11-3:10). What about David? He started out as a shepherd when he was anointed to become the next king of Israel (1 Samuel 16:1-13). Where they started didn't even compare to where the Lord took them and what He accomplished in their lives. In both cases it wasn't because of their own ability, but because the Spirit of the Lord was the One guiding and empowering them.

The bible is filled with countless examples of when God has called people to do more than what they thought they were able or qualified to do. However, it's important to remember and know that what we do, we don't do in our own ability. If God wills it, it will be done (Isaiah 55:11). He is the One that makes mountains as flat as plains before us. He is the One who can take our small beginnings and orchestrate things to reveal and magnify His glory and power over our lives and in the Earth.

Challenge: Mindset matters. Next time you find yourself faced with a situation that feels bigger than yourself, choose what you magnify. You can choose to make your situation big in your mind, or you can choose to acknowledge the bigness of God over everything you face. Rather than being overwhelmed by the mountain ahead of you, remember that it was God who created the mountain.

XXII.   DIRECT MY STEPS

Bucket lists. Journals. Vision Boards. These are just a few examples of ways we track and organize what we want to do in our lives. It's how we describe our dreams. Dreams help propel us forward and can be used to help determine a direction we want to move toward in our lives. They give us hope for what can be. Whether it's getting the degree, becoming an artist or visiting a national park, we all have things we want to do in our lives.

Proverbs 16:9 says "A man's heart plans his way, but the Lord directs his steps." Solomon, the writer of this proverb, was known for his wise and understanding heart. The Lord blessed and gifted him with the ability to understand things in a way that others could not (1 Kings 3:12). Being blessed by God with wisdom Solomon made the declaration that people are filled with dreams for how they want their life to look, but only God can make those ideas reality. Only the Lord can set us on a path that allows us to actually live out the dreams we purpose in our hearts.

We are told that hard work and grit is all we need to achieve. However, how many times can you count where you put in the effort and things didn't play out the way you planned? The same can be said of the opposite. How many times in your life were you given something that you didn't work for or that you didn't see coming. There is a verse in Matthew 5:3 where Jesus says to a crowd "Blessed *are* the poor in spirit, for theirs is the kingdom of heaven." When you think of being "poor in spirit," you can associate it with coming to the end of yourself. It's about being aware of ourselves. It happens when we acknowledge and realize our inherent need for God to be our Savior. When you think of inheriting the "kingdom of heaven," you can relate it to coming into all the things that God has planned for us in our lives.

I believe that in order for us to really live out the plans in our heart, we have to recognize God's hand in it. There are too many people out there believing the lie that we can manifest all of our dreams solely on our own ability. When all that's *really* needed is to take that first step and realize the simple truth, which is we all need God. Not every dream we have is good for us. Not everything we want will benefit us. When we chase after what we want solely based on our desires, we are bound to come across some outcomes that are detrimental to our overall well-being.

Jesus said this: "I have come that they may have life, and that they may have *it* more abundantly." Right before that He warns in the same verse "The thief [enemy-Satan] does not come except to steal, and to kill, and to destroy" (words added for context) (John 10: 10). It isn't us against God. We don't have to fight God to get what we want, because what He wants is for us to have the best. However, there is a very real enemy, the devil, that we must be aware of and defend against because he is described as the father of lies. If left unchecked this enemy can have us believing that in order to really live life, we have to do it in opposition of God and His Word (John 8: 44 & James 4: 7). Jesus reminds us that the opposite is true. It's when we bring God into our lives and recognize and choose to do life with Him, that we start to step into our purpose.

Challenge: Have you acknowledged to God and to yourself that you need Him? What is the current dream you have that you have yet to accomplishment or reach? Have you asked and invited God to be in on the process with you? Ask the Lord if it aligns with His plan over your life. Ask God to change your heart and mind if it doesn't *ps* to give you peace and confidence to pursue after it if it does.

XXIII.   NEW WINE

"And no one puts new wine into old wineskins;
or else the new wine bursts the wineskins, the
wine is spilled, and the wineskins are ruined. But
new wine must be put into new wineskins" (Mark
2: 22). Jesus used this parable to describe what He
was doing with the bringing forth of a new
covenant. When Jesus spoke, he often challenged
the ways people thought or behaved. Before
Jesus, people had their own idea for how God
should be worshipped and what it meant to be
children of God. However, some of the mindsets
and actions they had didn't accurately align with
the heart of God. One example is when the
pharisees and scribes tried to use the law of
Moses to justify stoning a woman who
committed adultery (John 8: 3-7).

The words that Jesus spoke represented the "new
wine," while we could say that the "old
wineskins" represented the engrained way of
thinking and believing that the people of that
time had. Those two things could not coexist.
One (Jesus' word) would burst the other (laws

and religions of man). Instead, a "new wineskin" was required to hold "new wine." Water baptism, baptism of the Holy Spirit, receiving salvation and the ongoing process of sanctification are all representative of becoming a new wineskin able to hold new wine.

It's important to note the element of sacrifice present in this verse. You can't keep your old life and old beliefs and also accept and maintain a true right standing relationship with God. In other words, we can't choose to be both self-serving and God serving. We can't choose to continue doing things in life that we know the Lord has defined as sinful and also practice living out the words of God. The Bible puts it this way "Therefore, if anyone *is* in Christ, *he is* a new creation; old things have passed away; behold, all things have become new" (2 Corinthians 5: 17). The definition of holiness is to be set apart. We serve a holy God who cannot co-exist with sin.

Making the choice to choose God does mean you are making the choice to reject the things which aren't of God. There is a dangerous perception that we can have both God *and* actively pursue to preserve aspects of our sinful nature and that somehow God will be fine with that. The bible warns of the dangers of being lukewarm in our decision-making or trying to prioritize the things of the world with the same level of reverence that should be given to God alone (Revelations 3: 14-16 & Matthew 6: 24). A choice has to be made and there is a time limit to how long we have to make that choice. My prayer for you is that you choose the ways, laws and commandments of God. You have so much more to gain with God, than you lose by rejecting the things of this world. 1 Corinthians 2: 9 says "Eye has not seen, nor ear heard, nor have entered into the heart of man the things which God has prepared for those who love Him." Choosing God is worth more than anything you could choose or possess in this world.

Challenge: What is the "new wine" God is establishing in your life? What direction is He leading you or what word has He placed on your heart? What will it take to be able to acquire this "new wine?" What will you need

to let go of in order to make room for what God is doing in your life? Have you readied your heart to receive or are you desperately trying to hold onto what God has already asked you submit?

XXIV.   LOVE COVERS

There is no greater or truer definition of love,
than the love of God for us. When Jesus met with
His disciples for the Last Supper, He took a piece
of bread, blessed it, broke it, and told them to eat
it, which symbolized how His body would be
broken for us. Then he took a cup of wine, gave
thanks and gave it to the disciples to drink. The
wine represented the blood of Jesus and the
formation of a new covenant with us. He said
"For this is My blood of the new covenant, which
is shed for many for the remission of sins"
(Matthew 26: 28). Jesus chose to bless the fact that
His body would be broken and gave thanks for
His blood that would be spilled for us.

Jesus knew the magnitude and severity of all that
He was about to face. He knew he would be
beaten beyond recognition (Isaiah 52: 14),
mocked and made to take die for a crime he was
innocent of (Matthew 27: 27-31 & Matthew 27: 21-
26). After all of that, He would have to
experience His Father turning away from Him,
so that He could fully take on the price and

burden for every one of our past, present and future sins (Matthew 27:46 & 1 Peter 2:24). In that moment, knowing everything He would have to suffer and endure, He chose to bless and give thanks. There is nothing that I could write that would ever do justice to accurately describe the depth of the Father's love for us or the magnitude of Jesus' sacrifice for us, but I am reminded of a verse in 1 Peter 4:8, which says "And above all things have fervent love for one another, for "love will cover a multitude of sins."

Jesus' death and resurrection is the ultimate example of how love covers sin. Jesus became the perfect sacrifice. What He did made it, so we don't have to continuously make sacrifices and go through priests to atone for our sins. His sacrifice, His blood covers all of our sins. There isn't anything we could ever do that could ever repay or equal the gift Jesus gave us, but we can honor Him by having love for one another and allowing that love to cover a multitude of sins. Love is the driving force that allows us to move forward and live in this world.

For that friend or family member who has burned their last bridge, reached that dead end and has hit a wall with no way to return or restore the lost relationship, love steps in and opens a door; it creates a path and makes a way for them to regain what once seemed lost forever. Love Covers.

For that mistake you made, the hurt you caused, the way you let pride lead you to a place you were never meant to be, love humbles, heals and forgives; letting you know that even in your worst moment you still have access to the redemptive power of God's grace and mercy over and in your life. Love Covers.

For everything we could ever go through in life, for every obstacle, setback and trial, there is a steadfast always present love that will cover us in every situation. We are never too far gone. We are never out of reach of God's love (Romans 8: 38-39). Love really does cover a multitude of sins.

Challenge: There are many ways we can show love. We can love by serving one another. We can love by listening and taking the time to just be with someone. We can love by giving what we have to someone who may not have. The list goes on and on. Today, honor God's love for you by showing love to another.

XXV.   ABIDE

When I think of the word abide, I think of these
words: "remain," "stay with" and "be a part of."
In John 15 there are promises that Jesus gives us,
as assurances for what happens when we abide in
Him. Verse 4 says "Abide in Me, and I in you. As
the branch cannot bear fruit of itself, unless it
abides in the vine, neither can you, unless you
abide in Me."

Promise 1) If we abide with God, He will abide in
us. That means He will come and live with us,
walk with us, be with us. We will never be alone.

Promise 2) We will bear fruit. Vines are naturally
supposed to bear fruit, so when we think of this
in comparison to our lives, we could say that if
we abide in Jesus we will naturally do and
become what we are supposed to do.

Verse 6 writes "If anyone does not abide in Me,
he is cast out as a branch and is withered; and
they gather them and throw *them* into the fire,
and they are burned." Jesus is represented here as

a source of sustainability and life. If we are detached from our Savior, we cannot survive. However, He promises "If you abide in Me, and My words abide in you, you will ask what you desire, and it shall be done for you" (John 15:7). If we're truly abiding in the Lord and allowing His word to abide in us, then our desires will change and begin to reflect the desires of the Lord. When that happens, we pray in accordance with His will and He answers so that we may be fruitful in our lives. However, just as it takes time for a branch to bear fruit, it takes time for us to become familiar with the Word of the Lord in order for us to pray and petition the Lord in a way that reflects His will.

In John 15 verse 11 Jesus says, "These things I have spoken to you, that My joy may remain in you, and *that* your joy may be full." It's a beautiful thing to have a well of joy on the inside that never runs dry. That joy will be present with us, when we have lost a loved one, but we know that even as we grieve, there is joy in having loved and known that person at all. The joy of God will strengthen us when find ourselves facing yet another failure and feeling like our life is a series of mistakes. His joy will remind us that his love is steadfast, his mercies never end and they are new every morning (Lamentations 3: 22-23). That joy will stay with us and help to carry us through every moment of life. As we abide in the Lord, keep His commandments and allow His power to continue working on our hearts and in our minds, we will naturally find ourselves becoming more and more like Him.

Challenge: What is the last thing you remember reading or hearing about in God's word? How can you apply it to your own life?

XXVI.   CLEAN & NEW HEART

Repentance. Rededication. Renewal. All of these words have the common element of "coming back again." They involve the action of returning or starting over. When I think of the purposefulness of God, I feel immense gratitude that He considered and made a plan for the inevitable fact that we, as humans, would require some form of contingency plan for when we find ourselves in need of a fresh start or a do over. With the formation of the new covenant, we are no longer stuck on a road of sin which ultimately led to death (Romans 6: 23). Instead, God knew His creation well enough to know that, given enough time, we would find ourselves needing to repent, rededicate & be renewed.

There is a verse in Psalms 51: 10 that captures the essence of a prayer for repentance, rededication and renewal. It reads "Create in me a clean heart, O God, and renew a steadfast spirit within me." It reflects and compliments a later verse found in Ezekiel 36: 26, where the Lord tells the people of Israel "I will give you a new heart and put a new spirit within you; I will take the heart of stone out of your flesh and give you a heart of flesh." The first verse in Psalms 51: 10 reveals the speaker's realization of their need to repent. They recognized the necessity for a clean heart and that God was the only one who could provide that. Alongside this new heart, they also requested to be given a "steadfast spirit." The word steadfast, which is defined as unwavering, means that they didn't just want a new heart, so they could hit the reset button, make the same mistakes and then find themselves asking the Lord for the same thing later down the line. They wanted God to give them a spirit that would be persistently choosing the things of God. They wanted to pray in a way that they had assurances, that they wouldn't find themselves in a cyclical pattern of mess up, fess up, and then restart up.

The way the Lord responds to the house of Israel gives us a picture of how He responds to us, when we approach Him asking to be changed. God starts by saying He will give them a new heart and a new spirit. Then He promises to take the heart of stone out and replace it with a heart of flesh. When I think about the qualities of stone, it is hard, unyielding and if put under enough pressure it falls apart and breaks. However, flesh is flexible, capable of change, sensitive and able to grow. As we grow closer to God there are things that will change about the way we view ourselves, people and the world we live in. We recognize these things more and more as we become more sensitive to the Holy Spirit. In order to be sensitive to the Holy Spirit we need a heart of flesh.

We've all heard the saying that "people never really change." We use it to justify the actions of another *or* to give ourselves permission to give up on someone rather than putting in the work to walk through a difficult moment with them. The fact is the saying "people never really change" is an excuse, it's not a truth. Nothing is too hard or impossible for God (Jeremiah 32: 17 & Matthew 19: 26). God can give us a clean & new heart. He can make it so the addictions we once had, the mindsets we couldn't shake, the patterns of behavior that we once described as just "part of who we are" can completely change and shift. In exchange, He can give us a heart capable of hearing His voice when He speaks and being led by the Holy Spirit in all life matters.

Challenge: Do you have a habit, mindset or piece of yourself that you have accepted not because it brings you joy or fullness of life, but because you have lost hope that it will ever change? Ask the Lord to take it away and give you His best instead. You don't have to live holding onto what hurts you.

XXVII.   PEACE BE STILL

I think it's fair to say that if certain conditions were met, we could find ourselves in a situation where we are filled with fear and start to doubt or forget the things we once felt so secure and certain about. For example, having a job that provides one day and then being laid off the next or being healthy and then receiving a diagnosis that we didn't expect and aren't prepared in any way to handle, let alone accept. In Mark 4: 35-41, the disciples found themselves facing a crisis not unlike what we often face today. They were having an ordinary day, when Jesus gave the command for them to cross over to the other side of the sea and then soon found themselves caught in the middle of a great windstorm.

When things come at us so unexpectedly and so suddenly, it's easy to question God. We say and think things like: "Why me?", "Why is this happening?" or "If you *really* loved me, you wouldn't let me go through this?" In one moment, we can be praising God for His goodness and faithfulness and in the next with

105

the turn of the wind, we can be accusing and doubting if He ever really was good. In the disciples' case they chose to accuse Jesus and say "Teacher, do You not care that we are perishing?" (Mark 4:38). When they were put in a position where they had to face the storm, they made the fear-led choice to forget who was mightier than the storm.

Reading back over the story, I don't think many people would say the disciples' reactions were completely irrational. In fact, if we're honest with ourselves, I'd say many of us would admit that we'd react the same way if we were living back then and faced with a similar storm-like condition. However, there is a similar story in the bible where a boy found himself facing a giant and rather than running away in fear and denying everything he knew about His God, he decided to face his "storm" and declare who His God was. In 1 Samuel 17:45-47 David said this "I come to you in the name of the LORD of hosts…This day the LORD will deliver you into my hand…Then all this assembly shall know that the LORD does not save with sword and spear; for the battle *is* the LORD's" [abbreviated for purposeful context].

In both situations the disciples and David faced a crisis that was bigger than themselves and they knew they could not escape this trial unharmed without the intervention of God. However, the disciples that were with Jesus on the sea allowed their fear to become larger than their faith (Mark 4: 40). While David knew, even before facing his giant, that His God was mightier than anything He could and would ever face. It wasn't until Jesus "arose and rebuked the wind, and said to the sea, "Peace, be still!" that the disciples realized that their storm was under the command and the control of the Lord (Mark 4: 39).

In each story the Lord was with the people involved. Both times the Lord showed Himself mighty and able to save. Both the disciples and David experienced the omnipotence of God, but for one that revelation only came with hindsight, while for the other they went into their battle assured of who their God was and what He could do prior to knowing what the outcome would be. How we respond to a situation matters. God is the same regardless of how we react, but I want to be the type of person who goes through life confident in who my God is and not fearful of every unplanned and uncertain outcome.

Challenge: The challenges and trials that we face in our lives can reveal the condition of our hearts and bring to light the depth of our faith. Maybe you find that in your life your actions align more with the disciples on the boat. Perhaps when put in a situation that feels out of your control, you worry and fear about things that were never meant for you to control. It's never too late to pray and ask the Lord to help you see Him not as the God who created the storm, but as the God who commands the storm.

XXVIII.   IN ALL THINGS

One of the declarations that we can make of God
is that He is a provider. One excellent example of
this is present in Genesis 22: 1-14, where God
commands Abraham to take his son Isaac up a
mountain in the land of Moriah and offer him as
a burnt offering. If you have heard this story, you
know that Abraham didn't end up sacrificing
Isaac and instead the Lord provided a ram caught
in a thicket as a substitute. It's easy to remember
the happy ending and overlook what was being
asked of Abraham and the kind of faith that
would have been required to obey God.

When Abraham was given this word, He didn't
put it off or come up with excuses for why he had
to delay on doing what the Lord had
commanded. Instead, verse 3 says he "rose early
in the morning and saddled his donkey...to the
place of which God had told him" (abbreviated
for context). On top of that, the Lord asked
Abraham for his son, and not just any son either.
This was the son the Lord had given him as part
of a long-awaited fulfilled promise (Genesis

21: 1-3). You could say that Abraham was being asked what was of greater importance to him. Did he prioritize the blessings of his life or was the Lord higher than all of these things in his heart?

We could ask ourselves the same question. What really matters to us? What are we willing to walk away from or surrender in place of obeying, following and serving God? Sometimes we may find that we have placed things ahead of God. It could be that house, that job, that car, that TV show or that hobby. It isn't always tangible things either. Sometimes it's that prestige, that acknowledgement, our pride or our reputation. If we are put in the position and asked to choose God, to choose to obey what God is calling us to do or who He is calling us to be or where he is calling us to go, would we be able to leave the rest behind and obey?

It isn't an easy decision by any means, but I think we owe it to God and ourselves to ask if we have knowingly or unknowingly placed anything before God. When God provided Abraham with a ram to offer in place of his son Isaac, Abraham "called the name of the place, The-Lord-Will-Provide" (Genesis 22: 14). As Abraham grew old in age it's said that "the LORD had blessed Abraham in all things" (Genesis 24: 1). Abraham had chosen to put God first in all things and magnify Him greater than anything He had possessed, and he was blessed because of it. In fact, the world was blessed, because out of the line of Abraham came Jesus, the one who redeemed the world (Genesis 22: 16-18).

Challenge: There is always more to gain than we have to lose, when we follow after God and obey His word. It's easy to look at our lives and all of the things we have and struggle to choose Him over ourselves and what we think will provide and care for us. I pray that like Abraham each of us finds that as we make the choice to choose God through, above and in all things that the Lord reveals the glory and blessings that can be found in Him alone.

112

XXIX.   CAST YOUR CARES

Possessing the spirit of pridefulness can be described as having a willful and deliberate self-assured arrogance about oneself. Being prideful has a negative connotation in the bible. In 1 Peter 5:5 it says, "God resists the proud, but gives grace to the humble." Humility can be defined as having a correct awareness of oneself in relation to the greatness of God. You don't have to put yourself down or belittle yourself to be humble, but you do need to acknowledge *who* God is and honor and glorify Him for that.

Pridefulness can come from believing that everything we have in our lives, we accomplished or earned on our own. We did it. It was our own ability, gifts, talents, hard work and perseverance that got us there. Humility would look at the blessings in our lives and be filled with gratitude toward God for opening a path for us to receive that promotion or giving us favor to achieve a goal or job that we were unequipped and unqualified to receive. Humility always recognizes and thinks about the hand of God over lives and gives credit to the One who provides. The bible warns of the dangers of pride and exalting ourselves in place of exalting God. Proverbs 16:18 writes "Pride *goes* before destruction, and a haughty spirit before a fall." Luke 14:11 says "For whoever exalts himself will be humbled, and he who humbles himself will be exalted." The word of God is filled with verses cautioning about the consequences of allowing pride to reign in our hearts.

The bible is also filled with verses about the blessings that come with being humble. 1 Peter 5:6-7 says, "Therefore humble yourselves under the mighty hand of God, that He may exalt you in due time, casting all your care upon Him, for He cares for you." Reflecting on this verse, we could discern that there is a danger that comes with moving into situations before our time or without consulting the Lord beforehand. Inversely, there are also blessings that come with approaching the Lord with all the cares and worries we have in our life and looking to Him and not ourselves to fix it.

God cares about us. He knows the things that would be blessings in our lives and the right time for those blessings. He also knows the things that look good, but would only be temporary or become sources of burdens in our lives. If we go through life only relying on what we know and what we can do, then we are missing out on all the benefits and blessings that God desires for us to have. When we humble ourselves and seek Him first and throughout our lives, then we find that the heavy burden of trying to do everything on our own is lifted and we get to know God as the One who cares for us. The One who wants us to cast all our cares upon Him.

Challenge: What have you been carrying? What burden is resting on your shoulders? God is a Good Father who desires to meet and carry the needs of His children. It's okay to let go and let God be God in your life.

XXX.   REMEMBER ME

Have you ever thought about how you will be
remembered in this world? What will be said
about your life when everything is said and done?
Our lives consist of a series of choices. Some of
the decisions we make fill us with joy for
moments when we stood our ground for
something we believed in or chose to walk the
hard and often lonely path knowing it would lead
to strength of character. Then there are those
moments that we'd rather not think about too
much. Moments when we weren't our best selves
or the choices, we made didn't highlight the
people we wanted to be.

These choices, good or bad, culminated
something within us. Maybe they created a silent
resolve to do better next time. Perhaps they
revealed a part of ourselves that we didn't know
existed. Either way, what we do or what we don't
do shapes the perception of who others believe
we are. There are many who believe that
goodness is some sort of point system. If you do
more good than bad things, then you're in the

positive and you can be remembered as an overall good person.

How does God see us though? Does He determine our character solely on the basis of our own perceived "goodness?" In Psalms 25:7 David says "Do not remember the sins of my youth, nor my transgressions; according to Your mercy remember me, for Your goodness sake, O LORD." The often-unpopular truth is that we can never be "good enough" to equal up to God's holiness. No matter how many "good" things we do, we will still find ourselves slipping up and falling short, because we are human. You may find yourself asking "What's the point of even trying then?" However, the very fact that we are prone to make mistakes, is what allows us to be met with a merciful God who chooses not to judge and see us on the basis of our own goodness, but instead looks at us through eyes of mercy and grace, because of His goodness.

In Psalms 103:11-12 David writes of the Lord "For as the heavens are high above the earth, *so* great is His mercy toward those who fear Him; as far as the east is from the west, *so* far has He removed our transgressions from us." It isn't because of anything we've done or anything we could earn that allows us to walk through this life forgiven and free from our transgressions. It's because, when God looks at us, He sees us through eyes of mercy and grace; a free gift we have because of His son Jesus. That's not to say we have a get-out-of-jail free card with permission to do whatever we want, because "God will forgive us." No. God knows our hearts and the intention of our hearts, so while we may fool others, we can't fool God (Jeremiah 17: 10).

I believe the question we need to ask ourselves isn't "How will I be remembered in this world?" Rather, it's how will God remember me? I want to be remembered as someone who sought after God and was genuine in her pursuit of following His commandments and being obedient to everything He placed on my heart to do. I want to be remembered as His child, who accepted His son, Jesus, and received the gift of salvation. I want to see and remember myself the way God does and remember to see and remember others that same way as well.

Challenge: If there is an area of your life or decision you made that you regret that you have been holding onto or punishing yourself over, take it to the Lord in prayer. Confess with your heart where you have fallen short and ask the Lord to forgive you and to teach you how to accept that His forgiveness covers everything you could have ever done.

Sometimes it's hard to believe that it's really that easy to be set right again. We can feel like we need to go on walking in guilt and shame for a sin that God has already forgiven and covered in grace, but as the Psalmist says our transgressions are removed from us and remembered no more "as far as the east is from the west" (Psalm 103:12).

XXXI.   LION AND THE LAMB

Trying to fit God into a box of rules determined
by our own scope of knowledge doesn't work.
All throughout the bible, the Lord has shown that
He doesn't exist within our own constraints of
the laws of nature and science, but rather He
defies and defines nature and science itself to
align with His word and His law (Isaiah 55: 10-
11). Even the identity of Jesus is defined as
someone who is both lion and lamb. Those 2
things don't relate and yet both describe who He
is.

In Genesis 22: 8, there is a moment when
Abraham is speaking with his son Isaac about
what will be used as a sacrifice. Abraham says to
Isaac "My son, God will provide for Himself the
lamb for a burnt offering." Though the context of
this verse was in response to a question by Isaac
about why Abraham did not bring a lamb with
him if he and Isaac would be sacrificing to the
Lord, it also points to the future act of what God
did for us.

God could have required us to pay the cost of the consequences of our choices. He could have required us to sacrifice our own lives to fix the division we caused when we separated ourselves from Him in the Garden of Eden. This division was created when Adam and Eve ate of the Tree of the Knowledge of Good and Evil (Genesis 3). Instead, He provided His own son Jesus who is described as "a lamb without blemish and without spot" to be the sacrifice needed to cover our sins and restore and reconcile us and God (1 Peter 1: 19).

How then can someone sacrificed as a lamb, also be described as a lion? Many of the Israelite people of Jesus' time had their own idea of how, the Messiah, the promised Savior, would come. I highly doubt that many perceived that their savior would come as a sacrificial lamb. They probably had a more lion-like expectation of who God's Messiah would be. However, even though Jesus was human, He also held within Himself all the power of the Living God. Those 2 things might not sound like they could coexist, but that's only if we look at it through our own understanding of God, and not in the truth of who Jesus actually is.

Jesus chose to use His power not to save Himself, but to save us. There is a moment when Jesus is being tempted by the devil and the devil urges Him to throw Himself down from the pinnacle of the temple in Jerusalem. The devil tried to persuade Jesus to showcase His great power by saying, "For it is written: He shall give His angels charge over you, to keep you,' and, in *their* hands they shall bear you up, lest you dash your foot against a stone" (Luke 4: 10-11). Jesus resisted the right and power He had from God to save Himself in that moment. He did it again when He willingly allowed Himself to be crucified for our sins.

Lions are known for their might, power and authority. It can be said that one of the most lion-like things Jesus did wasn't a huge show of force and power to establish His glory for all to see. Instead, it was in how He restrained Himself from exercising the power He held all along and chose instead to use it for our benefit.

Jesus was offered up as a lamb for our sins and He rose again in power as a lion able to redeem all of creation. God doesn't exist within our limited view of what can and can't be in this world. However, that's a good thing. I personally want to serve a God who is able to do far more than I believe is possible or could ever imagine.

Challenge: The Lord is a big and powerful God. His power and might have no end or limit. Nothing exists outside of His capabilities. It's for this reason that we can find comfort in placing our hope in Him, because nothing is too mighty for the Lord.

XXXII.   A HIDDEN TREASURE

Can you think of something in your life so
important to you that its value couldn't be
measured by any numerical figure? It could be
tangible or something of emotional significance.
All that matters is that to you it's priceless. We
don't know what Heaven will be like or all that
awaits those who get the honor of going in. We
can only imagine what lies beyond the gates of
such a place. In fact, in 1 Corinthians 2:9 it is
written that "Eye has not seen, nor ear heard, nor
have entered into the heart of man the things
which God has prepared for those who love
Him." For that reason, I think it's safe to say that
there is more to life and our lives after this life
than we could ever fathom.

If you are anything like me, then maybe it's hard
to wrap your mind around something that feels
"far away" or in the "distant future" or it's just
easier to focus on your assignment on the earth
here and now. However, if God didn't want us to
at least contemplate and be aware of Heaven,
then He wouldn't have made it a point to talk

about it all throughout scripture. Knowing that Heaven exists and that it's possible for us to get there can give us hope, while we walk through the day-to-day moments of lives. Having hope is a powerful thing. So many times, it's the last defense we have right before feeling like giving up. Hope causes us to think in our lowest moments that "maybe just maybe, things will turn around and we can get out of this." Hope in Jesus is the most powerful thing, because it's placing your hope in the One who actually has the ability to save, restore and change everything.

Let me share a little hope with you about what awaits those who believe and trust in the Lord. Matthews 13:44 shares a short parable about the kingdom of heaven and it writes "the kingdom of heaven is like treasure hidden in a field, which a man found and hid; and for joy over it he goes and sells all that he has and buys that field." In this parable Jesus is giving the people a comparative view of what it is like to be children of God and receive access to the kingdom of heaven through the gift of salvation.

First, Jesus describes the kingdom of heaven like a hidden treasure. Meaning that heaven is to be associated with something of value and worth. Next, He says that when the man found the treasure he hid it. This could be symbolic of when you receive salvation and become knowledgeable about the truth of who Jesus is. You hide that truth deep in your heart, where nothing can steal it away from you or destroy it (Mark 4: 1-9; Mark 4: 13-20). Finally, Jesus says that the man was so overjoyed with what he found, that he sold all that he had and bought that field. When we know the true magnitude of the gift of knowing God, the things that we believed mattered so much don't compare with what we have in Him. Knowing Jesus is worth leaving our old lives behind, following after Him, meditating on His Words, and living His way.

Challenge: If you are reading this and you don't know God or have a relationship with Him yet, then please really take to heart the next words that I write. Give the Lord a chance. Get to know who God really is by reading His word. Search the bible and find

out more about what He wants to give you and
why He loves you; why He has always loved
you. Maybe you are reading this, and you do
know God. Take a moment to pause and
reflect on who God is and What He has done
in Your life. Sometimes in the busyness of life,
we forget to take time for the relationship that
matters most.

XXXIII.   IN THE BEGINNING

Take a moment and look around the space you
are in. What do you see? Do you see little pieces
of dust floating in the air around you? Is there
light pouring in from a naturally lit window?
What do you feel? Can you feel the breath in
your chest as you inhale and exhale? Do you
notice the light or heavy weight of the clothing
on your body or the pressure of the things under
or around you? The truth is our lives and the
space we live in are filled with things. Some are
big and some are tiny.

It's easy to find ourselves overlooking all of
these things that surround us, especially when
you consider how filled and occupied life can be.
However, God notices every small, unnoticed,
overlooked, perceivably insignificant detail.
After all, God is the creator of life itself. The
very first verse in the bible says "In the
beginning God created the heavens and the
earth." (Genesis 1: 1). The very first characteristic
we have of who God is, describes Him as a
creator. God creates. As you read further along in

129

Genesis, the scriptures detail the history of creation. It discusses how God created light, darkness, water, land, animals and eventually humankind. God created it all.

With so much unquantifiable time that has passed between now and the beginning of creation and all that we as humans have learned and experienced since then, it isn't hard to forget that just like there was a beginning, there is also an end to our time here on earth. In John 14:2 Jesus says "In My Father's house are many mansions; if *it were* not *so*, I would have told you. I go to prepare a place for you. And if I go and prepare a place for you, I will come again and receive you to Myself; that where I am, *there* you may be also." Right now, Jesus sits at the "right hand of God" in heaven (Mark 16:19). However, the day is coming when He will return.

It's important to not become complacent as we live out our lives here on earth. God's timing is not our timing. Our idea of "soon" is not His idea of "soon" and our perception of "long" is not His definition of "long." However, God is true to His word (Matthew 24:35). If He promised that He would come again, then He will come again. What seems like all the time in the world now, may prove to be gone in the blink of an eye, according to the timing of the Lord.

Revelations 16:15 compares the return of Jesus to the coming of a thief. Just like a thief, His return will be when we weren't suspecting it at a time that we do not know. Matthew 24:44 writes "Therefore you also be ready, for the Son of Man is coming at an hour you do not expect." It may not feel so urgent right now, but Jesus is coming again. Since we do not know how much time we have until His return, it's important to make the most of our time now.

Challenge: In place of complacency, we need to have an alert awareness about us. Instead of putting off what we hear the Lord calling us to do, imagine how much more effective it would be to follow through right away. Having regret in one's life for the things we wish we would've done is never enjoyable. I pray that you allow the Lord to build you up

**with courage to be obedient toward the things
He has placed in your heart to do.**

132

XXXIV.   GOD WITH US

One of my favorite names for Jesus in the bible is
Immanuel. It means "God with us." I have felt
alone many times in my life. I think one thing
that all of humanity has in common is that we
know what it is like to experience loneliness.
Loneliness isn't just quantified by the number of
people you have around you. You can be
surrounded by people in a very public place
doing something you love with people you love
and still feel alone and unseen. When God sent
His son down to earth, He spoke through an
angel saying that Joseph and Mary, his earthly
parents, should call Jesus' name Immanuel. It is
interesting that out of all the names and titles that
Jesus is recognized by "Wonderful, Counselor,
Mighty God, Everlasting Father, Prince of
Peace" (Isaiah 9: 6), the first name the Lord spoke
that He should be known by is translated to mean
"God with us" (Matthew 1: 23).

This reveals God's commitment to communicate
to the world the importance of who Jesus is to us.
He desired to show us that He is with us.

Although, the name Immanuel may have been new at the time, God telling His creation that He is with us is something He has repeatedly shown us time and time again. When Gideon went to war against the Midianites with only three hundred men carrying trumpets and pitchers with torches inside and was victorious in battle (Judges 7: 16-25) that was God with us.

When Moses demanded of Pharoah that He let the Hebrew children go and by the hand of God called down ten plagues until it was finally decreed that they could have their freedom (Exodus 7: 14-Exodus 12). That was God with us.

After Jesus was crucified and raised from the dead and His time on Earth was near an end, the Father gave us the Promise of the Holy Spirit, so that once we received the baptism of the Holy Spirit, we could access the authority and power of God's Spirit dwelling within us (Acts 1: 4-8). That is God with us.

All throughout scripture there is verse after verse and testimony after testimony of God saying to us that He is with us. Anything that speaks otherwise is a lie of the enemy, the devil. At the beginning of time in the Garden of Eden, God walked with His creation. When He gave us His son, Jesus, he named Him Immanuel meaning "God With Us." Because of the baptism and power of the Holy Spirit, we can confidently declare that we have God with us.

I think the message is clear. God wants us to know that no matter what we face, no matter how dark or hopeless the path ahead looks, we can have assurance and confidence in this: we are not alone. God is with us.

The gift of knowing and receiving the Holy Spirit is unfortunately not always taught, discussed or emphasized in many religious circles. The sad reality is that the value of the importance of the third part of the Holy Trinity has often been downgraded or left out completely. In John 16:7 Jesus said to his disciples "Nevertheless I tell you the truth. It is to your advantage that I go away; for if I do not go away, the Helper [Holy Spirit] will not come to you; but if I depart, I will send Him to you" (words added for context). The truth is that you

135

can't have a successful faith walk with Christ
and overcome the adversities of this world
without the power of the Holy Spirit living and
dwelling within you. The Holy Spirit teaches and
guides us in all truths (John 16:13-15). He helps
us in our weaknesses, makes intercession for us
when we pray and allows us to pray according to
the will of God (Romans 8:26-27). The Holy
Spirit is the reason we can stand on the Word of
God and say that "we know that all things work
together for good to those who love God, to those
who are the called according to *His* purpose"
(Romans 8:28).

**Challenge: Knowing God and knowing that it
is His desire to be with us can allow us to face
mountains and giants that we didn't think
possible before and come out the other side
victorious. Having God on our side is one of
the greatest gifts we can have as His children.
Take a moment and reflect on how God has
revealed that He is with you.**

XXXV.   FOR GOD SO LOVED THE WORLD

"For God so loved the world that He gave His only begotten Son, that whoever believes in Him should not perish but have everlasting life" (John 3: 16) is a verse that is familiar to many and often referenced to and used to reveal the character and love of God. This verse details the promise of God that we have that through His Son, Jesus Christ. It's easy to read or hear this verse and overlook the heart of God in it or be numb to enormity of what God did for us.

When it says that God "gave His only begotten Son," it's important to pause and note that this wasn't an easy sacrifice for God. This came at a great cost to God. He wasn't giving away something that He had an abundance of. He was giving away a piece of Himself, His only Son. Jesus wasn't some discarded pawn that was cast away without a second thought. In Matthew 3: 17 God says of Jesus "This is My beloved Son, in whom I am well pleased." Jesus was God made human. He had relevance to God. He mattered and was treasured by God. God allowed a piece of Himself to become human, so He could walk the earth as we did.

Our holy God allowed Himself to be put in a mortal vessel and experience hurt, pain, temptation, tragedy, loss and death as we do. God isn't some distant God that doesn't know what it's like to be human. He literally came to earth, so he could understand and experience exactly what it is like to live and walk on this earth, flaws and all. Hebrews 4:15 says "For we do not have a High Priest who cannot sympathize with our weaknesses, but was in all *points* tempted as *we are*, yet without sin." Basically, you can sum up that verse and say, "God understands what we go through and He understands what it means to be us." Every time you have felt pain, loss, fear, temptation and any other experience that comes with being human, God can relate because through Jesus, He felt it too. He loves us so much that He wanted to feel what we feel and walk through what we walk through.

To further understand the greatness of God's love for us, we have to remember that we are the ones who originally caused there to be separation between us and God. Adam and Eve's original sin of eating the fruit from the Tree of the Knowledge of Good and Evil set humanity on a crash course leading to our destruction and ultimate death. We severed the close relationship with God that He originally intended for us to have when He created us and placed us in the garden of Eden (Genesis 3). However, God didn't require us to solve and pay the penalty for the problem that we caused. No, instead it is written that "God demonstrates His own love toward us, in that while we were still sinners, Christ died for us" (Romans 5:8). God reconciled us to Him. He restored the broken relationship. He paid the price with His life and with His blood for our sins.

If there is one thing of value and importance I can leave you with it's this: the gift of salvation is freely given, but it was paid with a heavy price. It's a price we may never know the full weight or depth of, but because it was paid for us we can reap the insurmountable benefits of having life in Jesus Christ. Romans 10:9 says "that if you confess with your mouth the Lord

Jesus and believe in your heart that God has raised Him from the dead, you will be saved." Confession and belief are all that's required to accept the free gift of salvation and walk out of death from sin and into everlasting life in Christ Jesus.

Challenge: If you do not know Jesus as your Savior and you are ready to take that next step in faith towards having life and freedom in Him, then make the verbal confession of who Jesus is as Lord and believe in your heart that He is the son of God and that He was raised from the dead. I leave you with this verse and promise from the Lord "whoever calls on the name of the LORD shall be saved" (Romans 10:13).

Explanation of Referenced Verses

IV:

"Before I formed you in the womb I knew you; Before you were born I sanctified you; I ordained you a prophet to the nations."

Jeremiah 1:5 - God speaks to the Prophet Jeremiah to reveal to him just how purposeful God was in creating Jeremiah. God created, knew and had a purpose for Jeremiah before he was even born. Just like Jeremiah, God created, knows and has a purpose for each of us.

VIII:

"If we are faithless, He remains faithful; He cannot deny Himself."

2 Timothy 2:13 - An aspect of God's character is that even if we don't love Him, He will still love us. Even if we don't choose Him. He still chooses us. Even if we walk away from Him, He is faithful to us always. His faithfulness toward us doesn't change or fade away with time. He is faithful, regardless of whether we reciprocate His faithfulness or not.

"But God demonstrates His own love toward us, in that while we were still sinners, Christ died for us."

Romans 5:8 - God extended his love and mercy to us not because we were perfect or had it all together or were doing all the right things to be worthy of His love. He loves us right where we are and He was willing to die to show to prove it. That's the greatest kind of love: love displayed through action.

"And you shall know the truth, and the truth shall make you free."

John 8:32 - Once we know that God's Words are true and we make the choice to abide by them, we are able to access the power that comes with knowing the truth of this world. We don't have to be misled and destroyed by the lies present all around us, because we have knowledge through the truth of God. Knowing the truth, gives us the ability to recognize and discredit lies. Things we were once deceived by and things that once felt confusing and unclear are suddenly revealed in the truth of God. In that truth we are able to walk free from the deceptions that once hindered us.

XI:

"However, when He, the Spirit of truth, has come, He will guide you into all truth; for He will not speak on His own authority, but whatever He hears He will speak; and He will tell you things to come."

John 16:13 - The Holy Spirit, also known as, the Holy Ghost holds, knows and speaks all truth. He speaks directly the Words of God, which do not fail. The Holy Spirit will even reveal things that have yet to occur to those the Lord chooses to reveal that knowledge to.

"And I will pray the Father, and He will give you another Helper, that He may abide with you forever."

John 14:16 - The Holy Spirit comes from the Lord and He is given to us as a Helper. He is always with us wherever we go, because He abides with us forever.

"Teaching them to observe all things that I have commanded you; and lo, I am with you always, even to the end of the age.' Amen."

Matthew 28:20 - This verse is a promise and assurance we have from Jesus that He will be with us always and forever, even to end of life as we know it.

XII:

"Or what man is there among you who, if his son asks for bread, will give him a stone? Or if he asks for a fish, will he give him a serpent? If you then, being evil, know how to give good gifts to your children, how much more will your Father who is in heaven give good things to those who ask Him!"

Matthew 7:9-11 - We can have confidence that when we go to God our Father and ask Him for things that align with His character, Will and

Word, that He will give good things to those who
ask. All we need to do is ask.

XIII:

**"Therefore whoever hears these sayings of
Mine, and does them, I will liken him to a wise
man who built his house on the rock: and the
rain descended, the floods came, and the
winds blew and beat on that house; and it did
not fall, for it was founded on the rock. 'But
everyone who hears these sayings of Mine,
and does not do them, will be like a foolish
man who built his house on the sand: and the
rain descended, the floods came, and the
winds blew and beat on that house; and it fell.
And great was its fall'."**

Matthew 7:24-27 - This verse is a reminder that
the storms of life will come for all of us here on
earth. However, when we go through life's
difficulties with the Lord, we will not be
destroyed. If we try to face every trial without the
presence and power of God leading and holding
us up, we will only find that the things that come

against us will overtake us and what once stood solid and firm within us will be destroyed.

XIV:

"Peace I leave with you, My peace I give to you; not as the world gives do I give to you. Let not your heart be troubled, neither let it be afraid."

John 14:27 - When Jesus departed this world, He didn't leave us behind scrambling to pick up the pieces of living in a world without the King of Kings to guide and protect us. He sent us the Holy Spirit. The Holy Spirit's teaching allows us to remember Jesus' Words. His Words rests on our hearts and gives us assurances and a peace that cannot be shaken or taken away.

"Enter by the narrow gate; for wide is the gate and broad is the way that leads to destruction, and there are many who go in by it. Because narrow is the gate and difficult is the way which leads to life, and there are few who find it."

Matthew 7:13-14 - This verse shines a light on the truth that there are many ways to walk away from Jesus and walk towards our own destruction. Unfortunately, there are many who will walk this path knowingly and unknowingly. However, there is a way that leads to life. Jesus is the one and only way to life.
Anything else is a lie and will only lead to our destruction.

"Do you not believe that I am in the Father, and the Father in Me? The words that I speak to you I do not speak on My own authority; but the Father who dwells in Me does the works."

John 14:10 - This verse reveals that Jesus' authority was given to Him from God His Father. The words Jesus spoke, the works He did, He did them all at the command and the authority of the Father. Jesus and God the Father are one. Jesus is the narrow gate that leads to God. He is the second part of the Holy Trinity-Father, Son & Spirit.

**"For by one offering He has perfected forever
those who are being sanctified."**

Hebrews 10:14 – This verse reveals that Jesus'
one-time sacrifice was all that was needed to
allow us to be perfected forever through the
lifelong process of sanctification.

**"Therefore Jesus also, that He might sanctify
the people with His own blood, suffered
outside the gate."**

Hebrews 13:12 – This verse reveals that it is the
power of the blood of Jesus that allows us to be
sanctified.

**"Sanctify them by Your truth. Your word is
truth."**

John 17:17 – This verse reveals that as we read
and meditate on God's word, truth is revealed to
us through His word and that truth sanctifies us.

John 16: 13 - See earlier for explanation of scripture.

John 14:16 - See earlier for explanation of scripture.

XIX:

"Create in me a clean heart, O God, and renew a steadfast spirit within me."

Psalms 51:10 – This verse shows that the Lord has the ability to give us a clean heart and a steadfast (unwavering) spirit. We need God to work on, change and give us a new heart and spirit in order to really live out a life of obedience that aligns with the love and will of God. It isn't something we can accomplish on our own, it's only by God's power that it can be done.

"And do not be conformed to this world, but be transformed by the renewing of your mind, that you may prove what is that good and acceptable and perfect will of God."

Romans 12:2 - We can either be changed by this world or we can change our mindsets to reflect what is good, acceptable and perfect in God's eyes. Rather than live how the world lives we need to ask God to transform us to see and live things His way.

XX:

"Fear not, for I am with you; Be not dismayed, for I am your God. I will strengthen you, yes, I will help you, I will uphold you with My righteous right hand."

Isaiah 41:10 - God is our strength and our help. He holds us up and because of this promise we don't have to be afraid, because God is with us.

"But God, who is rich in mercy, because of His great love with which He loved us,"

Ephesians 2:4 - God can be thought of as a friend who chooses to use His great love to love us.

"The eyes of all look expectantly to You, and You give them their food in due season. You open Your hand and satisfy the desire of every living thing. The Lord is righteous in all His ways, gracious in all His works. The Lord is near to all who call upon Him, to all who call upon Him in truth. He will fulfill the desire of those who fear Him; He also will hear their cry and save them."

Psalms 145:15-19 - God delights in us. He delights in providing for us. He delights in being near to those who call upon them. He delights in saving us and fulfilling and satisfying our desires. A desire that can only be filled and met in Him.

"If we are faithless, He remains faithful; He cannot deny Himself."

2 Timothy 2:13 - Jesus is a friend who will always remain faithful to us, regardless of whether we reciprocate that love and faithfulness back to Him. His faithfulness is always given and never conditional.

"Behold, I stand at the door and knock. If anyone hears My voice and opens the door, I will come in to him and dine with him, and he with Me."

Revelation 3:20 - Jesus is not distant and waiting for us to catch up to Him or chase Him down. He's right here with us, knocking and wanting to come and have a relationship with us. He's patiently waiting for us to hear His voice and open the door to Him and let Him into our hearts and lives.

XXI:

"So shall My word be that goes forth from My mouth; it shall not return to Me void, but it shall accomplish what I please, and it shall prosper in the thing for which I sent it."

Isaiah 55: 11 – This verse speaks to the authority and power of God's Word. When the Lord speaks, it is impossible for nothing to happen. The moment He releases a Word from His mouth, what He says will be done.

XXII:

"You are of your father the devil, and the desires of your father you want to do. He was a murderer from the beginning, and does not stand in the truth, because there is no truth in him. When he speaks a lie, he speaks from his own resources, for he is a liar and the father of it."

John 8:44 - This scripture accurately describes the workings of the devil. The devil is a murderer and a liar. The truth does not exist in him. He speaks lies that he himself created. He is the father of lies. It's important to know these attributes about the devil, so that we can accurately see and discern the truth from the schemes of the devil. In Jesus we are guarded and protected by the truth.

"Therefore submit to God. Resist the devil and he will flee from you."

James 4: 7 - This verse gives us a guide for what to do when we find ourselves tempted or facing the lies and accusations of the devil. First, we must submit ourselves to God. God is our helper. When we go to God and make the choice to resist and stand against the lies of the devil, the enemy will flee.

XXIII:

"No one can serve two masters; for either he will hate the one and love the other, or else he will be loyal to the one and despise the other. You cannot serve God and mammon."

Matthew 6:24 - This verse specifically refers to trying to love both God and money equally. You can't love both, because you can't equally prioritize both. God must be higher and if he is not, then that means that you have made the love of money higher. It isn't just money, though. There shouldn't be anything that holds the same level of value as God in our lives. Not that dream, not that home, not that recognition and love from others, nothing should ever be equal to or higher than our love of God.

XXIV:

"Just as many were astonished at you, so His visage was marred more than any man, and His form more than the sons of men;"

Isaiah 52:14 - The prophet Isaiah prophesies of how God's future servant, Jesus, would be marred or disfigured more than any other man. It gives us a limited perspective of the magnitude of how much He was beaten and how He gave His body to be broken for our sins.

"And about the ninth hour Jesus cried out with a loud voice, saying, 'Eli, Eli, lama sabachthani?' that is, 'My God, My God, why have You forsaken Me'?"

Matthew 27:46 - While on the cross moments before His death, Jesus held all the sins of the world-past, present and future. God is holy and therefore cannot exist in communion with sin.

For this reason, in order for us to be reconciled with God, Jesus had to take all of our sins upon Himself and sacrifice His life for us to pay the cost of that sin. In doing so He made it so that we could be saved and live in freedom in Him. In order for this to happen, God had to turn away from Jesus and forsake the very Son He loved so dearly.

"Who Himself bore our sins in His own body on the tree, that we, having died to sins, might live for righteousness— by whose stripes you were healed."

1 Peter 2:24 - When Jesus bore our sins in His body as He died, our sin died with Him. Now we are in a New Covenant with God, where we can live in righteousness and receive healing through Christ Jesus.

"For I am persuaded that neither death nor life, nor angels nor principalities nor powers, nor things present nor things to come, nor height nor depth, nor any other created thing, shall be able to separate us from the love of God which is in Christ Jesus our Lord."

Romans 8:38-39 - We have unhindered everlasting access to the love of God through Christ Jesus. There is nothing that exists that is powerful enough to separate us from that love.

XXV:

"Through the Lord 's mercies we are not consumed, because His compassions fail not. They are new every morning; great is Your faithfulness."

Lamentations 3:22-23 - God's mercy toward us allows us to not be overcome by our own shortcomings in our lives. His compassion doesn't fail and it never runs out. Each morning we can wake up and feel comforted by the fact that God has a new fresh portion of mercy and compassion for us, because of His great faithfulness.

XXVI:

"For the wages of sin is death, but the gift of God is eternal life in Christ Jesus our Lord."

Romans 6:23 - To live in sin is to live in separation from God. When we are separated from God, we are separated from the promises and inheritances of God, like eternal life. Therefore, if we choose to live a life of sin we are choosing to take on the consequences of that sin, which is death.

"Ah, Lord God! Behold, You have made the heavens and the earth by Your great power and outstretched arm. There is nothing too hard for You."

Jeremiah 32:17 - God demonstrated that nothing is too hard for Him, when He created the heavens and the earth by His great power.

"But Jesus looked at them and said to them, 'With men this is impossible, but with God all things are possible'."

Matthew 19:26 - When the disciples are astonished at the difficulty and seemingly impossible probability of a rich man to enter the kingdom of God, Jesus reminds them that while these things may be impossible if they are sought after by man's ability alone, they are not impossible when done through the omnipotent power of God.

XXVII:

"But He said to them, 'Why are you so fearful? How is it that you have no faith'?"

Mark 4:40 - In this moment Jesus rebukes the disciples for forgetting who Jesus was and what He could do. They let their circumstance and the fear it generated override the confidence they had for who Jesus was. Their fear became greater than their faith.

XXVIII:

"And the Lord visited Sarah as He had said, and the Lord did for Sarah as He had spoken. For Sarah conceived and bore Abraham a son in his old age, at the set time of which God had spoken to him. And Abraham called the name of his son who was born to him—whom Sarah bore to him— Isaac."

Genesis 21:1-3 – God promised Sarah and Abraham that He would give them a child. It wasn't until they were old in age that Sarah gave birth to that promised son, Isaac. After years of waiting and believing in the Lord, the fulfillment of that promise must have given them great joy and gratitude toward the Lord. We can assume that Isaac would have been someone they both treasured, adored and loved.

"And said: 'By Myself I have sworn, says the Lord , because you have done this thing, and have not withheld your son, your only son — blessing I will bless you, and multiplying I will multiply your descendants as the stars of the heaven and as the sand which is on the seashore; and your descendants shall possess the gate of their enemies. In your seed all the nations of the earth shall be blessed, because you have obeyed My voice'."

Genesis 22:16-18 - When Abraham chose not to withhold any blessing or treasure he had from the Lord, the Lord swore upon Himself that He would bless and multiply Abraham. He continued to say that through Abraham all the nations of the earth would be blessed because of his obedience. Out of the line of Abraham came David and out of the line of David came Jesus. Jesus was and is God's greatest gift and blessing to this world.

XXX:

"I, the Lord, search the heart, I test the mind, even to give every man according to his ways, according to the fruit of his doings."

Jeremiah 17:10 · God has the ability to search our hearts and test our minds. Nothing about us is hidden from Him. We may be able to fool others and even ourselves, but we can never fool God. He knows us better than anyone.

XXXI:

"For as the rain comes down, and the snow from heaven, and do not return there, but water the earth, and make it bring forth and bud, that it may give seed to the sower and bread to the eater, so shall My word be that goes forth from My mouth; It shall not return

**to Me void, but it shall accomplish what I
please, and it shall prosper in the thing for
which I sent it."**

Isaiah 55:10-11 - When the Lord speaks a word,
all of creation, nature and the laws of science
respond in obedience to accomplish and
complete what He declares. We see it in Genesis
1:3 when God says, "Let there be light."; and
there was light."

XXXII:

Mark 4:1-9; Mark 4:13-20 - The first set of
verses detail a parable about a sower whose
seeds land in various places. Some fell by the
wayside, others on stony grounds, some amongst
thorns and some on good ground. The second set
of verses explains how the seeds represent the
Word of God and how only the Word that was
sown on good ground prospered and increased.
Having knowledge of the truth of God's Word
and hiding it away in our hearts, so that nothing
and no one could ever steal or destroy it can be
compared with viewing His Word as a hidden
treasure.

XXXIII:

"Heaven and earth will pass away, but My words will by no means pass away."

Matthew 24:35 - The world as we know it to be may pass away, but if the Lord declares something will happen, it will happen.

XXXIV:

"However, when He, the Spirit of truth, has come, He will guide you into all truth; for He will not speak on His own authority, but whatever He hears He will speak; and He will tell you things to come. He will glorify Me, for He will take of what is Mine and declare it to you. All things that the Father has are Mine. Therefore I said that He will take of Mine and declare it to you."

John 16:13-15 - The Holy Spirit is known as the spirit of truth. He is the third part of the Holy Trinity. He speaks only what He hears from God the Father (first part of the Holy Trinity). The Holy Spirit glorifies Jesus (the second part of the

Holy Trinity). He reveals things to come and declares them to us.